Participation

Concepts in Social Policy

General editors:

Vic George, Professor of Social Policy and Administration and Social Work, University of Kent

Paul Wilding, Professor of Social Administration, University of Manchester

Initiated to open up and broaden discussion of theory within the study of social policy, this new series presents texts covering concepts which have particular relevance to this field. Each text will analyse a concept or related concepts from theoretical and multi-disciplinary standpoints, and will discuss their usefulness to the development and practice of social policy.

The concepts to be covered will include:

PARTICIPATION
STIGMA
RIGHTS AND DISCRETION
RATIONING
POWER
PREVENTION

Concepts in Social Policy One

Participation

Ann Richardson

Routledge & Kegan Paul

London, Boston, Melbourne and Henley

First published in 1983
by Routledge & Kegan Paul plc
39 Store Street, London WC1E 7DD,
9 Park Street, Boston, Mass. 02108, USA,
296 Beaconsfield Parade, Middle Park,
Melbourne, 3206, Australia, and
Broadway House, Newtown Road,
Henley-on-Thames, Oxon RG9 1EN
Printed in Great Britain by
T.J. Press Ltd, Padstow, Cornwall

Library of Congress Cataloging in Publication Data

Richardson, Ann.

Participation.
(Concepts in social policy)
Bibliography: p.
Includes index.
1. Great Britain – Social policy. 2. Social
participation – Great Britain. I. Title. II. Series.
HV248.R52 1983   361.6'15'0941   83-3338

ISBN 0-7100-9469-8

Contents

Acknowledgments

Acknowledgments must be given, but where does one begin? I have been studying the general subject of participation for far too long to be able to give due acknowledgment to everyone who has contributed to this book's completion. I would need to acknowledge not only my colleagues in the research world for their comments and advice about participation in theory, but also those people in the 'real world' who put up with my questions about participation in practice. I would want to acknowledge not only all those who helped me to work on and understand this subject, but also all those helpers in the background, the unsung heroines of working mothers, who enabled me to work at all. I hope I have shown due appreciation in each relevant direction over the course of time.

With respect to this manuscript, however, I would like to thank the editor of *Policy and Politics* for allowing me to re-use some material first published in that journal. A few friends read an early draft; they know who they are and that I am grateful to them. Finally, while authors often thank their families for enduring a lack of constant attention, my own has shown no evidence of undue suffering as a result of this work. Some blame may, indeed, go the other way, but that is another story.

1 Introduction

Participation is a very old idea. Debated by political philosophers over the centuries, it falls on modern ears with little sense of novelty. The opportunity to take part is such a fundamental tenet of the democratic system of government that its very existence is rarely questioned. People must be able to have their say — to vote, to engage in political debate and to let those in power know their views on issues which concern them. This is what democracy is all about.

Yet participation has emerged as a new political issue. The adequacy of traditional means of enabling those who wish to play a part to do so has increasingly come under fire. It is said that the growth of the modern state, with its seemingly limitless layers of departments and committees, has made it more and more difficult for the individual voice to be heard. At the same time, both the number and nature of the issues with which the state has become involved make it even more imperative that ordinary citizens' views be expressed. There is a need, it is argued, for the old institutions to be reviewed, and new institutions created, in order to reassert the primacy of the idea of participation.

This book is about the potentialities and limitations of such new institutions in the context of social policy. It is not concerned to win any new converts to them, nor to foster their development, but simply to understand what they are all about. It examines the various arrangements which have been established to bring about greater participation in social policy issues, and considers what pressures have led to their development. It explores the many claims which have been made both for and against the introduction of these arrangements, and analyses the processes which they necessarily entail. No data are provided on how participation works in practice, or who participates and why; no recommendations are made about the best form of participation or how

1

to make it work more effectively. This book is solely concerned to explore the *idea* of participation; it is, unashamedly, abstract and analytical.

Calls for greater participation in the social policy arena have focussed principally on the recipients, or consumers, of statutory services. It is argued that they must bear the consequences of policy decisions, and therefore should be able to play some part in their formulation. Concern has thus been expressed that parents should be able to be involved in the government of their children's schools, that tenants should be able to take part in the management of their housing, that users of the health services should be able to have a say in their provision, and so forth. It is the participation of these groups in discussions about their services with which this analysis is primarily concerned.

There are two other groups who cannot be entirely omitted from the discussion, however. First, some argue that it is not solely the direct recipients of services who should be involved, but the wider community — anyone, in fact, who wishes to be so. Lots of people are affected by decisions even if they are not the direct beneficiaries, and they too, it is said, should be able to express their views. Secondly, some interest has also centred on the potential for worker participation in the social policy context. It is argued that employees of statutory services should have the same opportunities for involvement as their counterparts in some areas of the private sector. They too, after all, are affected by policy decisions, in having to carry them out.

Both the meaning and the application of participation are very much the same in all these cases. The arguments for getting people involved — and for limiting their involvement — are no different with respect to workers or the general community than when raised with respect to consumers. The institutions through which these groups can be enabled to participate are identical as well. Indeed, the processes of participation do not change because different people are participating. This book focusses on consumer participation in order to provide a clear theme and line of argument. It would be unduly obtrusive to refer to all groups, or to shift between groups, throughout the discussion. None the less, it should be seen as an analysis of the concept of participation in whatever context it is found.

The idea of consumer participation is a relative newcomer to the agenda of social policy. Certainly the founding fathers of the current welfare state, both in Britain and elsewhere, never felt called upon to address it at all. Traditional concern in this area focussed on identifying the most effective policies for any given service and ensuring that they were adopted and implemented in practice. The methods by which these policies might be developed received scant attention; the key issue was not how they were devised or who was involved in doing so but what emerged in the end. The consumers were assumed not only to have little interest in policy deliberations but also little capacity for contributing effectively to this process. It was up to the experts – the professionals, politicians and managers – to ensure that consumers' needs were well served. The limitations of this arrangement from the consumer's point of view was not an issue which aroused much concern.

In the late 1960s, and throughout most of the 1970s, however, this situation changed dramatically. There was a sudden upsurge of interest in the idea that ordinary citizens might have a part to play in the decision-making process. In many different countries, and at many different levels, this idea found expression in demands for participation in a myriad of new contexts. Along with citizens in other capacities, the consumer of statutory social services was no longer to be viewed as the passive recipient of decisions made by others on his behalf. He could actually be involved in framing social policies and influencing their character. Participation had arrived as a significant component of social welfare.

In Britain, the widespread acceptance which the idea of participation had achieved was reflected in discussions of every single area of social policy. No service remained untouched by this interest. Indeed, all the enquiries into the administration of individual services which took place during this time gave some attention to this issue. In 1968, the Seebohm Report on the reorganisation of the local authority personal social services urged the new Social Services Departments to consider how clients might be more involved in decision-making and service delivery. In 1974, the reorganised National Health Service introduced the Community Health Councils, set up to provide a means for consumer representation in health service administration. In 1977, the Taylor Committee, established to consider arrangements for school management, recommended greater parental involvement on governing boards. In the same year, the Housing Review carried out by the Department of the Environment urged the implementation of systems for tenant participation in council-housing management. Consumer participation in both of these areas, education and housing, was also subsequently the focus of legislation (in 1980). Even in the one area of social policy where the 'consumer' might be thought to be weakest, the supplementary benefits scheme, an enquiry was carried out in 1977 into the feasibility of 'user' participation. Finally, although not traditionally viewed as an area of social policy, environmental planning has been the target of perhaps the greatest attention with respect to participation, fuelled by the passage of legislation in 1968 and the publication of the Skeffington Report on exactly this subject in 1969.

The sheer extent of this interest makes it difficult to appreciate that its genesis is so recent. The causes of this change in climate are not easily traced, and surprisingly little attention has been given to this question. It can be argued that it derives from fundamental changes in public attitudes to authority, making people no longer willing to accept decisions made by others on their behalf. But it may equally derive from changes in the nature and structure of service provision. The growth in the size of governmental institutions has distanced those who make decisions from those on whose behalf such decisions are made, and this has brought in its wake pressures to reduce this distance by a variety of means, including participation. There have also been changes in the numbers of service consumers, and in the extent to which they have become organised, and these, too, may have played some part.

Whatever its origins, participation has proved a controversial infant on the social policy scene. One of the more striking features of discussions on this issue is the widely varying assessments participation has received. It has aroused considerable passion among both its advocates and its critics, and created some strange bedfellows. Little consensus has been reached about what participation actually does, for the new participants or for anyone else. Highly incompatible claims exist side by side concerning the direction of its impact and its implications for policy.

When demands for greater participation were first introduced into discussions of the organisation of social services, the general climate of informed opinion was largely favourable to them. Official decision-makers, whether elected or appointed, were judged to be too remote to understand the needs of the ordinary consumer. It was felt that those affected by decisions should be able to exercise some influence over policies, to ensure that their perspective was not lost in the cumbersome process of deliberation. The introduction of some system for involving consumers provided an obvious route to this end. Not only was it seen as a key means of ensuring fair processes, and creating better decisions, but the act of participating would also bring greater fulfilment and understanding to those involved. Participation, like motherhood, was clearly A Good Thing.

But times, and climates of opinion, change, and participation (along with motherhood) began to be challenged from a number of quarters. Some critics, noting the extent to which it was taken up by persons in positions of authority, argued that participation was just a clever 'con', increasing the legitimacy of those making decisions without any concomitant diminution in their overall power. The participating consumers would be co-opted by the system, they argued, reducing the influence of the consumer population, instead of increasing it. Others questioned the extent to which the participants could or would be representative; if participation benefited only the more organised and articulate, they suggested, the interests of the wider community might be better served through more traditional political institutions.

The student of social policy should not be surprised by the presence of conflict or controversy; it is the stuff of which all political issues are made. But divergent opinions about the aims to be achieved are one thing; conflicting interpretations of the direction a policy will take are quite another. If some argue that participation is a significant means of increasing the influence of the new participants, and others contend that it is instead a devious means of decreasing it, someone must indeed be incorrect. These are logically incompatible analyses of ostensibly the same phenomenon. Either they are talking about different things, in which case further clarification is necessary to enable the discussion to continue, or they are misunderstanding the thing itself. One must begin to ask, in short, what participation is all about.

The aim of this book is to provide some answers to this question. It is based on the premise that people are talking about the same thing, but have failed to appreciate the nature of the processes it entails. Participation has been put into practice with many different structures, and with many different intentions, but it remains none the less a single phenomenon. The conflicting claims which have been asserted both in its favour and against it do not arise from attention to different 'kinds' of participation, but from inadequate understanding of the thing itself. Amid the reams of rhetoric which have been produced on this subject, there has been a dearth of serious analysis. This book represents one attempt to rectify this situation.

Participation is approached here as a single phenomenon not only in terms of its many forms but also with respect to its many contexts.

This book is not about participation in housing, or education or planning as such. With the exception of some brief attention to the specific forms it has taken in these and other areas of social policy, and to the origins of the idea in these contexts, it is concerned to explore the nature of participation in all of its manifestations. It attempts to provide a single vocabulary for discussing participation, drawing together the general themes which underlie its discussion in disparate policy areas and calling attention to the common issues and controversies between them. Once viewed in this way, the parallels in the literature, not only between different service areas but also between consumers, workers and the general community, are striking.

A brief overview of the plan of this book may prove helpful. Chapter 2 establishes a general definition of participation and considers the various forms it can take in practice. Chapter 3 gives brief attention to the ways in which it has been implemented in Britain in each of the major substantive areas of social policy — health, housing, education, the personal social services and social security — and adds environmental planning to this list. Chapter 4 considers the claims which have been made both for and against the introduction of participation, the arguments on which it has been advocated and opposed. Chapter 5 analyses the processes which participation entails and reviews the claims of the preceding chapter in the light of this analysis. Chapter 6 is devoted to the question of why participation became such a popular theme during the last decade. Finally, Chapter 7 ventures some speculation about the future role of participation and presents some considerations toward its evaluation.

One note of terminology must be appended here. Because this book is written for readers with a wide range of interests, potentially distracting references to specific groups or institutions have been avoided as much as possible. Instead, only very general terms are used, which can be applied to any context of interest to the individual reader. The term 'consumer' thus refers to all those on the receiving end of social services: tenants, clients, parents and so forth.* Similarly, the term 'decision-maker' (or 'policy-maker' or 'service-provider') refers to all

---

* The term 'consumer' may be thought somewhat inappropriate in the context of statutory social services, since while the recipients use or consume these services they do not necessarily pay for them, and certainly not directly as with consumer goods. Unfortunately, there is no obvious alternative; the word 'user' is accurate but awkward and uncommon, and the word 'recipient' and its synonyms carry pejorative overtones.

those who typically make decisions about services, whether appointed or elected: housing managers, social workers, teachers, administrators, local authority councillors and so forth. Finally, the term 'social services' refers to all areas of social policy provision, including (somewhat idiosyncratically) environmental planning. It is hoped that the potential awkwardness of this terminology will be offset by the level of generality it enables the text to achieve. In the same way and for the same reason, the exposition refers primarily to consumer participation, although employee participation or that of the general public is, as mentioned above, readily encompassed by it.

2 The concept and forms of participation

The aim of this chapter is to establish what the term 'participation' means and what it is that people participate in when they participate at all. But one might well ask why there should be any need for more than a cursory definition. Surely, to participate means to take part, to become involved, and there is little more to it than that. And, in the context under discussion here, the general area of social policy, participation refers to the ways in which ordinary citizens can or do take part in the formulation or implementation of social policy decisions.

But it is not quite as simple as that. Certainly, the term 'participation' refers to taking part in some activity with other people; the *Oxford English Dictionary* defines it as 'a taking part (with others) in some action or matter' and that seems clear enough. But arguments quickly arise, even within the relatively limited territory of social policy, about what 'taking part' really means. Does it require involvement in decision-making itself or only some input into the process by which decisions get made? Does it require the exercise of some influence? Where does participation in pressure groups, or even in the electoral process alone, fit into this discussion? Given the existence of society, everyone participates in a wide range of activities with other people; the only non-participator is the person whose life is entirely autonomous, a hermit. But not everyone participates in the processes of formulating or implementing social policy. It is therefore necessary to establish boundaries, to clarify who is defined as taking part, with which others and in what activities they are collectively engaged.

Participation and social policy

What, then, is meant by participation in the context of social policy? Before the specific forms which this can take are explored, some attention must be given to delineating the territory under discussion. First, what does the word 'participation' imply for purposes of this analysis? While the definition given above assumes some action on the part of the participant, the term is occasionally extended to include a state of mind. Participation under this usage is contrasted to apathy; a person is said to participate in an issue or event when he is actively concerned about it, whether or not he takes any action to demonstrate this concern. While this meaning is subsumed in any definition of participation entailing action, the reverse does not similarly hold: if a person is involved in an activity, his mind is generally also so engaged, but there can be no presumption of action solely because there is concern. This 'mental' usage of the term should be noted here, but no further attention will be given to it. Throughout this study, participation is taken to imply some action on the part of the participant.

But action alone is also not enough. Again, participation can be defined in terms of undertaking some activity – doing something instead of doing nothing. Following this usage, a person is said to participate in an activity as long as he is not inactive, whether or not anyone else is involved. There are clearly a number of ways in which an individual may find his own solution to a problem without recourse to others, and in doing so may be seen to be fully involved in it. But participation as used here entails more than taking individual responsibility for some action. It implies sharing in an activity, undertaking activities with other people.

Second, what is meant by 'social policy'? This is an elusive concept to define, and no attempt to do so will be offered here. It has come to be associated with certain statutory services traditionally viewed as contributing to social welfare, and it is easiest to accept these as the territory under discussion. They are, quite simply, health services, housing, education, the personal social services and social security, and, for purposes of this analysis, environmental planning is added to the list. This is not to argue that other state activities do not contribute to social welfare (nor that these necessarily do), nor that the concept of participation cannot be equally applied to such other areas. These boundaries are set primarily for the reader's (and writer's) convenience, to focus the discussion. The analysis would apply equally in other areas of statutory activity.

When people participate, then, they engage in activities relating to the provision of a range of social services by central or local government. What these activities are, and with whom they are undertaken, are explored at length below. It can be said here that they concern the processes of policy formulation and execution and are usually entered into in order to influence their course. Participation in social policy means the introduction of a new set of people into the public policy-making process.

But many may argue, quite rightly, that social policy is not solely the province of the state. Activities to increase social welfare are undertaken in addition by voluntary organisations and groups, by commercial institutions and by individuals for one another on a voluntary or paid basis. And, indeed, participation in these activities could be seen as participating in the formulation or implementation of social policy. This view would be strictly correct, although somewhat idiosyncratic in most of these contexts, given normal usage of the term, but to give it full attention would serve to deflect attention from the principal focus of this study. Those interested in these other areas can draw their own parallels.

It must be noted that these boundaries expressly exclude one form of 'participation' which is commonly labelled exactly by this term — involvement in a variety of voluntary associations, including mutual-aid groups and consumer co-operatives. There are a growing number of organisations, comprised of people with a common interest or problem, which provide both help and support to members entirely outside the statutory sector. These include not only housing and food co-operatives but also many groups focussed on particular medical and social conditions, such as stroke clubs and widows' groups, in which members try to help each other solve common problems. The involvement of members in these organisations is rightly seen as a form of participation, since they take part both in joint discussions and in activities to help one another. It may furthermore be seen as participation in social policy, since the associations themselves are concerned with members' social welfare. Indeed, the processes of — and benefits from — participation in these groups may bear considerable similarity to those of participation in the statutory sector. But the two circumstances are not identical, either in terms of who is involved or with respect to the ramifications of their involvement, and they should not be confused. It is participation with officialdom, focussed on the services they provide, with which this discussion is primarily concerned.

Forms of participation: (i) indirect

Participation finds expression in many different forms. People engage in activities concerned with statutory social policy in many different ways. To assist analysis of these forms, it is useful to introduce one fundamental distinction, that between *direct* and *indirect* participation. Direct participation refers to all those means by which people take part in efforts to influence the course of government policy involving personal (face-to-face) interaction with official spokesmen. Indirect participation refers to those means by which people take part in such efforts but not involving personal interaction with these spokesmen. This book is primarily concerned with arrangements for direct participation, the 'new institutions' for participation as they were termed in the introduction. None the less, it may help to clarify the subject if some brief attention is first given to the forms and functions of indirect participation.

Indirect participation basically consists of all those activities which are commonly known as ordinary 'political participation', together with some new activities of a similar nature made necessary where arrangements for direct participation have been introduced. Political participation has been rather loosely defined as 'those legal activities by private citizens that are more or less directly aimed at influencing the selection of government personnel and/or the actions they take'.[1] Such activities traditionally include voting, campaigning on behalf of particular candidates or issues and taking part both in political parties and in pressure groups. They are not generally directed solely to social policy issues, since their impact is necessarily broad, but participation in such activities can, of course, affect social policies and may be undertaken in order to do so. The 'participants' are all citizens who wish to become so involved, and there is usually no selection process for participation (unless one counts electoral registration). The 'others' with whom the individual participants are involved are solely their peers, other people like themselves who choose to vote, campaign or take part in other forms of political activity. There is no direct involvement, by definition, with government officials.

Arrangements for indirect participation are inherently necessary in all modern democracies, since not all citizens can play a direct role in the business of government. Some system of representation is required, and therefore some system for selecting the representatives. The whole issue of representation has been the focus of much philosophical discussion, and while a long digression into this territory is not appropriate here, a few relevant issues may be noted. The principal problem for any system of representation is the inherent impossibility for one person, or set of persons, to speak for the exact concerns of a larger body. This is not solely because the representative may find it difficult to learn what his constituents' views are; more fundamentally, the latter may not have a consistent set of views or, especially with respect to new issues, may have no articulated views at all. Even where these problems do not arise, constituents may have insufficient information or have given inadequate consideration to the ramifications of an issue, so that their expressed views are not consistent with their underlying interests. In consequence, the dilemma is often posed of whether representatives should attempt to reflect their constituents' articulated concerns or, alternatively, to use their own judgment to discern their constituents' real concerns.

The means by which representatives are selected, and how they are interpreted, can be seen to have some bearing on this question. The selection procedure may be viewed as a mechanism for constituents to authorise their representatives to take particular positions, for instance where specific issues have been raised in the course of the selection process. It may alternatively be seen as a means of enabling constituents to hold their representatives to account, showing by their selection or rejection that positions already taken were or were not considered appropriate. On a somewhat different plane, the selection procedure may also affect the characteristics of the people chosen; it may facilitate the selection of 'typical' representatives, reflecting certain critical characteristics of the constituents, or 'untypical' ones, who may none the less prove equally or more able to articulate their constituents' concerns.[2]

Most of these issues are not normally raised in the course of everyday political debate; the existing arrangements for political participation, and the philosophical and practical issues underlying them, tend not to be questioned. Pressures for change do emerge from time to time, however, arising from perceived inequities in the political system. Demands for proportional representation, for instance, can be interpreted as evidence of dissatisfaction with the degree to which the electoral system reflects participants' (voters') wishes. Similarly, the debate about the means of selecting the Labour party leader can be seen to stem in part from concern about the appropriate role of participating 'activist' constituents in their local party. (Both issues should also be interpreted as arising from political demands of specific groups, and not simply concern over abstract issues like participation, but that is another matter.) But while occasional debates may arise about the appropriate structures and institutions for political participation, it is generally accepted that citizens should be able to take part in order to influence the course of those representing them.

Participation in pressure groups, while viewed as a form of normal political participation, differs from voting and other political activity in being much more specifically focussed. Not aimed simply at indicating a general desired direction (more welfare services, less interventionism), it is seen as a means of gaining particular changes in policy. Pressure groups come in all shapes and sizes and focus, of course, on many different sorts of issues. Groups concerned with specific statutory social services have been on the increase in recent years, both at national and at local level. There are organisations focussed on broad groups or services as a whole, such as the Child Poverty Action Group and the National Tenants Organisation, and those focussed on individual local areas or institutions, such as estate-based tenant associations and local parent groups.

For the individual member, participation in pressure groups can vary from the simple payment of dues to active involvement in committee work and the mobilisation of other members into political action. Furthermore, the activities in which the groups themselves engage may range from entirely peaceful tactics to illegal and disruptive ones. There has recently been an upsurge of academic interest in various forms of protest behaviour, called 'aggressive political participation'[3] or 'unconventional political behaviour'[4] but the activities of most pressure groups are not so dramatic. They generally consist of publishing pamphlets or policy statements, mobilising correspondence with elected representatives and organising the occasional demonstration. Involvement in all these activities should be viewed as forms of indirect participation.

But in addition to these means by which individuals can make an active effort to influence the course of government policy, there are other less traditional means by which their views can be solicited, which also represent forms of indirect participation. Referenda on particular policy issues, for instance, should be viewed in this light, enabling citizens to channel their collective response to those who must take an eventual decision. Social surveys have also been increasingly employed for this purpose, focussed in some cases on the general population and in others on specific groups within it. They can provide a wealth of detailed information on individuals' views, including those of consumers of particular services or in particular areas. Both these methods of collecting information are, of course, limited to the provision of a static picture of public opinion at a given time. More fluid mechanisms may be developed, however, through the application of new technology, the computer and coaxial cable, to this problem. It may prove possible for members of the public to maintain regular contact with their representatives, responding to their actions and registering their opinion of particular decisions.[5] The development of such systems would greatly expand the scope for indirect participation in social, as well as other, policy-making.

Finally, consumers can participate indirectly in similar ways as described above to influence the course of specific institutions established for direct participation. Just as the democratic process limits the participation of most citizens to indirect means, so too do most systems for direct consumer participation. It is simply not possible for everyone to take part. The general population of consumers may thus be involved in selecting their spokesmen in these arrangements, campaigning on their behalf or engaging in activities to influence their positions on particular issues. Similarly, the views of ordinary consumers may be solicited by those who represent them, by surveys or other means. All of the means of indirect political participation outlined above can be equally applied to the specific context of systems for consumer participation.

Forms of participation: (ii) direct

The bulk of the interest in participation in social policy is directed, however, not to the functioning of indirect participation, but to the operation of systems for direct participation. These comprise all those means by which consumer spokesmen are brought into direct personal contact with elected members or appointed officials for mutual discussions. Most interest centres on arrangements which are officially sanctioned and formally established, but they may also be unofficial and informal. Schemes may also be set up on a regular basis or they may take place only at irregular intervals. Wherever and however consumers meet the service providers to discuss their service provision, direct participation can be said to take place.

Unlike indirect participants, the direct participants are inevitably limited in number by the sheer practicalities of time and space; only so many people can be seen in a day or fit into a meeting room. Where participation has been formally instituted, there is generally a formalised selection procedure to designate specific, named, spokesmen. This may entail an election in which all affected consumers can take part or particular groups or associations may be asked to designate their own representative, either by appointment or by some system of internal election. In other words, mechanisms for the indirect participation of the majority of consumers, as discussed above, tend to be brought into play. Where participation is less formalised, however, the participants may not necessarily be designated individuals; they may even be self-appointed, as in the case of public meetings where any interested person may go and make his opinions known.

Whereas in the case of indirect participation the participants take part only with each other, in the case of direct participation they take part both with each other and with official spokesmen for the service in question. These are, separately or together, the elected members or appointed officers who, in the absence of any participation arrangements, would be solely responsible for decision-making or service delivery. In a few exceptional cases, however, they may have been brought into discussions because of the introduction of consumer participation, in order to represent an 'official' point of view. Such officials may also be consumers of the services under discussion; local authority councillors, for instance, are often council tenants or parents of children at local schools. But while the widespread use of the statutory social services may blur the distinction between providers and consumers in practice, the analytical distinction is clear. The service providers may well have an interest in issues *as* consumers, and this may indeed affect the outcome of discussions, but they can be readily identified as spokesmen for the 'official' side.

But what do the participants actually do? What are the activities in which they are engaged when they take part in arrangements for direct participation? First, consumers may take part in the delivery of particular services. This means, quite simply, that they are involved in some way in the actual provision of help either to themselves or to others in their situation. They become, in other words, both givers and receivers of care or assistance. While many forms of help require the co-operation of the person receiving it, for example in attending clinics or classes, participation entails something more than this. The recipient must be actively involved in helping to give support, advice or particular services along with those who normally do so.

Consumer participation in service delivery is relatively rare in the case of most statutory social services. There are occasional exceptions, such as where pupils assist teachers by taking classes, parents help out in council-run playgroups or where able-bodied pensioners in residential homes provide some services to other residents, but it is essentially a marginal phenomenon. Indeed, it has aroused little interest among either consumers or providers of services, although attention is occasionally drawn to the subject in official or other reports.[6] Little further attention will be given to it here.

Secondly, consumers may take part in the decision-making process about the provision of their services. This forms the principal focus of recent interest in the idea of participation and is the mode of participation with which this analysis is primarily concerned. It entails some form of meeting between consumers and those who determine service policies, to enable decisions to be discussed between them. Such meetings may take place at many different levels and under many different formal arrangements, depending in part on who the decision-makers are and in what forum they normally carry out the business of decision-making. But while consumers may be invited to take part in existing committees or discussion meetings, new arrangements may also be devised to accommodate them. These various forms of participation must be considered in turn.

Where consumer participation is effected through existing structures, its nature is necessarily constrained by their particular form. Services vary considerably in the structure of their decision-making, but there are two general locations which are particularly relevant here. First, there are the institutions through which policies are developed on an overall basis for service provision in a given area. These are typically centralised, for an entire local authority or the country as a whole, but they may be decentralised to smaller units, such as districts within an authority or regions of the country. Second, certain decisions may be devolved to those personnel responsible for providing the service at the point of delivery, in other words the individual hospital, school or housing estate. Consumer participation may be established at either level.*.

* One can also speak of 'participation in decision-making' on an individual's own case — a patient with his doctor or a client with his social worker. This is clearly more a matter of professional relationships than institutional arrangements for general policy-making, although this analysis remains relevant.

In both cases, the formulation of general policies for a given area and the development of specific policies for a given institution, there are typically one or more committees whose established purpose is to hold discussions about — and eventually decide — the nature of the services to be provided. In the former situation, these committees generally comprise those people who have been elected to carry out the business of government: Members of Parliament or local authority councillors. A ready example is the housing committee of a local council. In some circumstances, however, these committees instead comprise people who were appointed for this task, although some may be elected members of their local authority. An example here is a regional health authority. In the latter situation, the point of delivery, committees are generally composed only of appointed members, including staff of the relevant institution, although again some may also be elected members of their local authority. The governing boards of primary and secondary schools provide one example here. Not all such committees have executive (decision-making) powers, but they are set up to provide an arena in which discussions about the service in question can take place.

It can be seen that one obvious forum for introducing direct consumer participation is the relevant committee or sub-committee for the particular service. Council housing tenants have been invited to sit as co-opted members of some local authority housing committees or management sub-committees, parents have been co-opted on to education committees and so forth. Similarly, at the level of individual institutions, consumers can be invited to take part in local management committees. Parents have thus been appointed to school governing boards and residents have been involved on management committees of old people's homes. In general, the consumers who are so involved are given the same powers as all other members, but there are some cases where they are invited to attend meetings but not allowed to vote.

But some view these formal, and largely statutory, committees as inappropriate vehicles for consumer participation, both because only a few consumers can be involved and because only some of the issues with which they are concerned are seen as legitimate subjects for consumer influence. Instead, it is argued that new committees should be established for the express purpose of consumer participation, comprised largely of consumers and focussed entirely on issues relevant to them. Various consultative and advisory committees have therefore been set up to discuss housing, planning, health and other issues. These do not have any formal decision-making powers, but can feed recommendations into the policy-making process of the relevant authority. They may be established centrally or on a decentralised basis, enabling particular attention to be given to specific local areas.

The involvement of consumers in all such committees, whether statutory or *ad hoc*, is a means of establishing formal consumer participation in the policy-making process. By providing an institutional forum for regular discussions between consumers and decision-makers, committees are readily identifiable mechanisms for ensuring consumers a voice in the formal deliberative process. But they represent only one part of the potential for consumer participation. Just as many decisions are taken, officially or otherwise, outside of formal committees, so too consumer participation can be effected through other channels. Methods of informal participation include any systems by which discussions are facilitated between consumers and decision-makers outside a formal committee structure.

One means of implementing informal participation in some subject areas is a public meeting. Having a less formal status than a committee and involving a smaller commitment to regular interaction, a public meeting none the less enables consumers and decision-makers to pursue issues of common interest to them — or of interest to one or the other. Such meetings may be open to anyone who wishes to attend or they may be limited to those who can show that they are consumers of the relevant service. Like the consultative committees noted above, such meetings do not have any formal powers, but they too can play some part in producing suggestions or recommendations to be put to decision-makers in other forums. In certain circumstances, such meetings may be statutorily indicated, and have clearly specified functions, as in the case of public enquiries in the planning process.

But consumers can also play a direct part in decision-making by even more informal means. In all social service contexts, it is not uncommon for consumers to get the attention of decision-makers, at one level or another, for private discussions. While many such private meetings focus on individual cases, others concern general issues of policy or service delivery; indeed, even individual cases often have more general ramifications. These discussions often occur on an *ad hoc* basis, such as a delegation which presents some immediate problem to the relevant authority, but some officials invite consumers to meet them regularly to review ongoing matters. Although such arrangements are not typically public and therefore not readily identifiable, they should none the less be recognised as forms of direct consumer participation in decision-making.

In between these two extremes, the wholly public meeting and the wholly private one, there are many other sorts of arrangements for discussions between decision-makers and consumers. Conferences and seminars on particular policy issues have increasingly encouraged the attendance of some relevant consumers to represent their point of view to the professionals and politicians present. Indeed, it is not unknown for consumer spokesmen to be asked to give a formal presentation on such occasions, and to be available for questions as 'experts' on their particular service. Such meetings can be developed into regular occasions, enabling an exchange of views to take place on an annual, or even more frequent, basis.

It should be noted that direct participation in decision-making as defined here does not automatically imply membership of a decision-making body. Consumers are said to participate whenever they are involved in discussions with those involved in the decision-making process. Even within the restricted context of formal participation in committees, it is not assumed that the consumers necessarily have full membership status or that the body in which they are involved has full executive powers. Of course, consumers may be co-opted as voting members on to a committee with such powers, and this is defined as participation. But equally, consumers may be invited to submit their views to a meeting with no decision-making powers and this is also defined as participation. It is the simple interaction of consumers and policy-makers which represents the key defining variable for this analysis.

But having identified the many forms of direct consumer participation in decision-making, it is necessary to establish the activities in which the consumers might be expected to engage. The activity of participation is not synonymous with the activity of taking decisions, and at least some of the confusion which surrounds this whole subject derives from failure to appreciate this simple point. Participation in decision-making means participation in the process by which decisions are made. Many different activities are encompassed by this process and participation may take place in any one – or all – of them.

While decision-makers do not always approach their task in a fully systematic way, it is still possible to outline the steps which they tend to follow, whether systematically or not, in the course of their deliberations. In principle, they must define the issues or problem for consideration, amass appropriate information about the consequences of alternative courses of action, establish their collective priorities or goals and adopt a particular position. Once a decision has been taken, someone may be responsible for overseeing its implementation and assessing its results. These various tasks may be undertaken by the decision-making body as a group or they may be carried out by individual members on their own. All are parts of the decision-making process, but any of them — including the taking of a decision at all — can and often will be omitted in particular circumstances.

When consumers participate in the decision-making process, they may be involved in any one or all of these activities. They may be asked to help define the issues needing resolution, for instance not only what sort of car park is provided in an area but whether one should be provided at all. They may be asked to provide speculation on the consequences of different decisions, such as the likely usage of a garage by local residents or the expected rate of vandalism in its absence. They may be consulted about their own priorities, and the uses to which any resources saved might be put. Finally, they may be entitled to vote on the final decision. On the other hand, consumers may be invited to take part in only one stage of this process, and given no say in any voting which subsequently occurs. As long as they are there at some point, interacting with those who make decisions or those who report to them, some participation can be said to take place.

It should be stressed that a very broad range of decisions is covered by this discussion. Some, like the car park example given above, are very specific and practical. Others, however, may be at a much more general level, for instance whether car parks should be built at all by the authority and under what circumstances. Others, still, will concern more abstract matters, such as whether there should be a set of regulations governing conditions of tenancy and who should be involved in defining them. On a completely different plane, some decisions will involve relatively small sums of money, whereas others will entail the expenditure of considerable resources. Some will concern all consumers of the service, whereas others will affect only one group, either functionally or geographically defined. All form part of the great variety of decisions likely to be taken with respect to a given service over a given time period.

Not only are there many types of decision in which consumers may become involved, but there are also many different points at which they may be brought into the decision-making process. This is not simply because there are a number of different locations at which decisions can be made, as already noted above. It must be recognised that decisions which have in principle been firmly taken may get reviewed in the course of their transmission to those responsible for putting them into practice. A council may adopt a particular broad policy, which appears clear enough, but someone must then interpret whether the appropriate conditions do in fact prevail. The decision to implement may be delayed, due to various pressures or demands on resources, and the implementation itself may also be delayed, even extensively so, for similar reasons. Participation in decision-making may be most readily visible at the beginning of this cycle, where the policies are framed, but it may prove equally important at its more disjointed reaches, where they are put into practice.

It has been stated at the outset, but it should perhaps be reiterated, that this entire discussion, while framed in terms of the consumer, applies equally to the case of worker or general public participation in the statutory sector. These groups, too, may participate indirectly or directly, and the structures through which they might do so are the same as described above. They, too, may take part in the ordinary political process and in pressure group (including union) activities. They, too, may be invited to participate in formal committees, whether with executive powers or of an advisory nature, or in informal arrangements for participation, such as public meetings and conferences. Finally, the activities in which they might engage are the same as analysed here, ranging from providing some limited input into the decision-making process to voting on the decisions themselves. They have been omitted from this discussion solely to keep the exposition clear.

Related concepts

Having established at some length what participation in social policy *is*, it may be useful to clarify, at least briefly, what it is *not*. There are various governmental arrangements which are commonly associated with participation, but should be distinguished from it. The decentralisation of administration, for example, is often described as a means of bringing government services closer to their consumers, enabling them to be more fully involved in them, but it does not in itself entail any form of consumer participation. Consumers may have no greater contact with decision-makers under a decentralised structure than under a centralised one. When accompanied by any of the devices described here, such as local advisory bodies involving consumers or regular meetings between officials and consumers, decentralisation may encourage or facilitate participation. But the two concepts should not be confused; consumer participation may be effected under both centralised and decentralised management structures.

Similarly, the employment of community workers to develop and liaise with voluntary groups is commonly viewed as a means of bringing about a greater closeness between service consumers and providers, but again it does not in itself ensure any consumer participation in decision-making. The issue here is not lack of contact, for the precise job of the community worker is to develop good working relations with consumers and their organisations. But community workers are not policy-makers; they are junior employees with relatively little access themselves to the policy-making process. Where their employment is accompanied by the introduction of arrangements for consumer participation, they may assist consumer groups to participate effectively and offer them moral and other support. But the existence of community workers should not be equated with consumer participation; they do not and cannot be said to institutionalise participation solely by their presence.

Thirdly, in some circles the development of more open government through widespread publicity about government policies and practices has been claimed as a form of consumer participation. Such publicity, whether via leaflets or newsletters or through public exhibitions, enables consumers to be better informed about existing and future policies, but it does not in itself provide a means of consumer participation. Unlike social surveys, which filter consumers' views to policy-makers, government publicity entails communication solely in the opposite direction. Unless it is accompanied by mechanisms to solicit consumers' reactions to it, publicity gives consumers no particular role in the policy-making process. It may be a useful adjunct to consumer participation, but should not be equated with it.

Finally, full consumer control over services, whatever their origins in the statutory sector, is quite distinct from consumer participation, although frequently linked to it. This is a relatively rare phenomenon, but there has been considerable interest in its potential, for instance the development of tenant co-operatives from former council housing. In such cases, the consumers may well be fully involved, participating in the administration of their service, but there is no equivalent input from the statutory side. Their participation in this case is identical to that of members of any private association run as a collective. They do not need to share the decision-making process with anyone else besides their peers.

Participation and power

The definition of participation put forward here is ostensibly a very simple one. It has been described as the introduction of a new set of actors into the various processes or activities of policy development or delivery, entailing their involvement with others in them. With a few rare exceptions, these activities would be undertaken in any case without the new participants. Most social services would be provided, in other words, whether or not any consumers are actively involved in their delivery. Similarly, decisions about these services would be taken whether or not any consumers play any part in the process of formulating or implementing them. Indeed, the relevant decision-makers would be subject to a number of influences regardless of the role played by consumers in this respect. Consumer participation in any of these processes may well affect their outcome, and may additionally affect the views of the people involved, but the processes themselves are not changed in any essential way by its introduction. At its analytically simplest, participation means the addition of a new set of people into a particular situation.

In fact, of course, the introduction of a new set of people into most situations is not a simple matter. It upsets the balance of relationships which had existed before their arrival and calls for new arrangements to be devised, whether formal or informal, for accommodating the new participants. New demands may be made, new considerations raised and old alliances upset by the introduction of new people. The nature of service delivery may be subtly or radically changed by ideas brought in by the new participants. Similarly, the nature of discussions about decisions, as well as the decisions themselves, may be subtly or radically changed by the presence of new participants. The processes may indeed be the same, but their dynamics and consequences may well be affected dramatically by the introduction of participation.

It must be noted, however, that no presumption of such change is built into the definition of participation provided here. In this respect, this analysis differs sharply from many other interpretations of this phenomenon. A number of writers, including many of the key contributors to the literature in this area, have attempted to distinguish 'true' participation from lesser imitations on exactly this basis. In particular, they have been concerned to exclude those circumstances where the participants have no effective influence or power. This is a critical issue for further analysis, and it requires some attention.

In his recent writings on political participation, for example, Sidney Verba explicitly qualifies this subject to exclude what he calls 'ceremonial' or 'support' participation. These are defined as those situations 'whereby citizens "take part" by expressing support for the government, marching in parades [etc]'.[7] The basis for this exclusion is clearly stated: 'the kind of participation in which we are interested . . . emphasises a flow of influence upward from the masses.'[8] This concern can also be found in his earlier writings on participation in the small-group context. He coined the term 'pseudo-participation' to refer to procedures by which members are induced to agree to decisions already taken, suggesting 'participation is in most cases limited to member endorsement of decisions made by the leader. . . . As used in much of the small group literature, participatory democratic leadership refers not to a technique of decision but to a technique of persuasion.'[9]

Carole Pateman, another central writer in this field, also follows this path, but takes it one step further. In her discussion of worker participation in industry, she explicitly disparages the sort of neutral definition provided here; she writes, 'the whole point about industrial participation is that it involves a modification, to a greater or lesser degree, of the orthodox authority structure.'[10] After excluding 'pseudo-participation' as defined by Verba from her terrain, she proposes a two-fold definition of participation based on the degree of power open to the new participants. 'Full participation' is defined as 'a process where each individual member of a decision-making body has equal power to determine the outcome of decisions'; 'partial participation', in contrast, is defined as 'a process in which two or more parties influence each other in the making of decisions but the final power to decide rests with one party only.'[11] Some of the difficulties entailed by these definitions are given passing mention in a footnote: 'in practice in any particular case it might be difficult to distinguish the situation where actual influence does occur from the pseudo-participation situation, where it does not. But the theoretical distinction is clear.'[12]

A similar attempt, employing different terminology, is made by

Geraint Parry in his writing on political participation. Following a discussion of the effectiveness of participation in achieving the goals of the participants, he puts forward the concept of 'unreal' participation. This is defined as the circumstance 'where [participation] is a mere facade because the decisional outcome is structurally predetermined'.[13] Like Pateman, he recognises that this definition can incur problems, stating, ' "unreal" participation shades into ineffective participation and the boundary is difficult to determine'.[14]

There can be little argument with the proposition that the concept of power is crucial for analysing the impact of participation in practice, for it 'flows in every nook and cranny of interpersonal and social life'.[15] But its incorporation into a definition of participation does little to aid understanding. These writings, while seeming reasonable in the first instance, serve to illustrate this problem. It is not only exceedingly difficult to trace the existence of power or influence in practice but also it is at best inconvenient to define situations according to their assumed outcome. Following the strict definitions offered by these writers, the existence or absence of a participatory situation cannot be established without information on its results. Their concern to emphasise the dimension of power, in fact, obscures the very real uncertainty of the direction it may take.

In addressing this problem it is useful to draw a distinction between the notion of 'power' and that of formally established 'powers'. The latter is fairly easily defined in terms of the formal responsibilities delegated to any particular group. A local authority has certain statutory powers conferred by Parliament; a council committee similarly has certain powers delegated by the council as a whole. All decision-making bodies have formally defined terms of reference, establishing the boundaries of their authority; their powers comprise the issues over which they may make decisions without recourse to ratification or amendment by others. Similarly, the members of such bodies have formally defined powers, which may vary between them; some committees, for example, have both voting and non-voting members. Although the degree to which committees have legally defined powers differs from one context to another, it is generally possible to establish what these powers are.

Establishing the existence of power, on the other hand, is not so simple. A person can be said to have power in a specific context when he can determine a particular outcome, ensuring that, in ordinary parlance, he gets what he wants. It follows from this that a group of people have power when they too can determine outcomes, ensuring that they get, as a group, what they jointly want. But unlike the formal powers described above, this power can be neither legislated nor ensured; it is the outcome of a complex process of negotiation between different individuals or groups.

For the analyst of participation, along with all other forms of political activity, a real problem arises when efforts are made to identify those with power. Political scientists have wrestled with this issue in the context of decision-making for many years and have derived a number of disparate responses. Many propose that power should be investigated by careful study of particular decisions, enabling it to be ascribed to those who are successful in gaining their own ends.[16] Others contend that this procedure obscures the power to keep issues off the political agenda; it is necessary in addition to investigate 'non-decision-making', whereby issues which involve 'a latent or manifest challenge to the values or interests of the decision-maker' are suppressed or thwarted.[17] A third view suggests that these procedures for studying behaviour ignore the subtle ways in which people can and do influence each other's actual wishes; as one proponent of this position writes, 'is it not the supreme exercise of power to get another or others to have the desires you want them to have . . . ?'[18] The identification of power, following this view, requires the recognition of the 'real interests' of those affected by it, which may not only not be expressed but also may not even be consciously felt.

This very brief résumé of different approaches to the study of power has been introduced here to illustrate the very real difficulties likely to be encountered in any attempt to identify its presence. In addition, however, it can be seen that power is not an attribute that can be established by an examination of formal structures or functions; it can only be identified (if at all) after careful study of particular events. In the context of consumer participation, one can examine decisions taken, trace issues which never reached the relevant agenda, and even surmise about the 'real interests' of the various participants in terms of such issues, but these are all difficult and time-consuming exercises. None of these procedures should be required in order to define participation or to identify those circumstances in which it exists.

Of course, participation schemes do differ in the degree of formal powers open to the participants. Some committees have few delegated powers and some systems for participation in committees do not give full membership status to those consumers involved in them. Perhaps, it might be argued, it is these circumstances which the writers quoted above are concerned to exclude. But to do so is to fail to recognise the significance of the distinction between formal powers and actual power. Although the exertion of the latter may be more difficult in the absence of the former, it is by no means impossible; a wide range of options are open to the participants to employ to persuade those with formal powers to their point of view. It simply cannot be assumed that participation is ineffective, or unreal, or partial, on the sole grounds that formal powers are lacking. The key dimension for a definition of participation should not concern power at all; it is the existence of access, and therefore interaction, between the groups involved.

It should be stressed that by excluding the concept of power from the definition of participation, it is not being suggested here that it is an insignificant variable for understanding how participation works. On the contrary, the exercise of power is an integral part of any interaction which takes place between consumers and decision-makers, whether or not they consciously recognise this fact. But the direction in which it is exercised, who is able to get what they want from whom, cannot be established *ex ante*; it must be identified (if indeed it can be identified) only after particular decisions have been taken. Assertions about the degree of power held by the participants should be framed not as elements of a definition of participation but instead as hypotheses about its results.

Summary

This chapter has shown that participation refers not to one mechanism or activity, but to many. In the context of social policy, it describes all those means by which those affected by statutory services take some part in policy formulation or implementation. While this analysis is focussed primarily on the participation of consumers in social service provision, it can also be applied to the involvement of employees or the wider community in such activities. Participation can be direct, entailing personal contact between the participants and policy-makers, or indirect, entailing efforts by the participants to influence policy without such contact. It can take place in the delivery of services or in the decision-making process by which these services are devised. There are many different ways in which participation can be effected, ranging from formal membership of committees to informal contacts between those affected by decisions and those responsible for their formulation. Participation should not be defined, however, in terms of the degree of influence it brings about; this must be studied as one possible effect of participation, not its essence.

3 Recent initiatives in participation in social policy

As the main purpose of this book is analytical, it might be tempting to avoid any reference to the ways in which participation has been implemented in practice. But as it is often easier to relate theory to actual rather than hypothetical arrangements, this chapter provides a brief overview of current systems for consumer participation. This covers the five major areas of social policy concern — health, housing, education, the personal social services and social security — as well as the general area of environmental planning. A brief section on employee participation in these areas is also included here. It focusses solely on developments in Britain; no effort has been made to provide information on participation elsewhere. Anyone already familiar with this material, or uninterested in it, can turn to subsequent chapters with no loss of theoretical argument; a few general issues are summarised, however, at the end of the chapter.

The introduction of formal arrangements for consumer participation is a very recent phenomenon in this country. Indeed, as noted in the Introduction, the sheer extent of practical developments in this area in a short space of time is striking. Little interest had been expressed in the idea before the late 1960s, yet from that time to the present proposals were put forward for consumer participation in every one of the substantive areas mentioned above. Not all of these proposals have been implemented, and some have received only limited expression. None the less, the current scene includes a wide range of examples of consumer participation in practice.

It is impossible in a single chapter to do justice to these many developments, and the following discussion must be viewed as only a cursory introduction to this subject. With respect to each social policy area, a brief outline of the structure of decision-making is provided, followed by a review of the major ways in which consumer participation in it has been implemented, or in a few cases only advocated. Attention is given only to formal systems for direct participation in decision-making, and details are provided of their structure, functions and methods of selecting the participants involved. While some comments are offered on the genesis and subsequent history of these arrangements, the question of why these schemes have generally come to be developed is explored more fully in Chapter 6. In order to avoid an interruption of the general exposition, further reading is provided in the bibliography at the end of the book.

Health

Statutory responsibility for providing health care to the general population rests primarily with the National Health Service. While medical services are delivered by hospitals, family practitioners and miscellaneous other groups (e.g. dentists, opticians, etc.), they are administered by two separate sets of health authorities under the supervision of the Department of Health and Social Security. These are the regional health authorities, responsible for general oversight and co-ordination, and the locally based district health authorities. A middle tier, the area health authorities, was eliminated in 1982. Members of the regional health authorities are appointed by the Secretary of State, with a proportion nominated by local authorities and a proportion by health service staff. Members of the district health authorities are appointed by the regional health authorities, with some local authority and some NHS staff nominations. At both administrative levels, executive responsibility rests in a management team, comprised of senior medical, nursing and administrative specialists. In addition, there is a wide range of advisory bodies in operation at national and local levels.

The idea of consumer participation in the administration of the health service has been given formal expression in two separate sets of structures. First, there are the community health councils (CHCs), introduced at district level to speak for health service consumers when the NHS was reorganised in 1974 (and similar bodies, differently named, in Scotland and Northern Ireland). Second, there are what have come to be called 'patients' participation groups' (PPGs), developed during the past decade around individual surgeries in a few areas. These are discussed below in turn. Although CHCs have been in existence for some time, arrangements concerning their operation have been somewhat revised by administrative changes in the NHS put into effect in 1982. This description is therefore based in part on existing experience and in part on what are, at the time of writing, future plans.

Since September 1982, there have been 217 community health councils in England and Wales, corresponding generally to the individual district health authorities. The membership of each CHC is roughly eighteen to twenty-four, with most falling at the lower end of this range. Half the members are nominated by the relevant local authority, one-third by local voluntary associations and the remaining one-sixth by the regional health authority. The members are not chosen because they are health service consumers as such, although as ordinary citizens they are likely to have used services from time to time, but they are expected to speak for, and represent the interests of, consumers. The local voluntary associations are expected to be 'interested in health matters' or in a health service institution, including the appropriate trades council. Most CHCs have two full-time staff, a secretary and an assistant, who are employees of the relevant regional health authority. Some have shop-front premises in popular shopping areas; others rent office accommodation from the local council or health authority. A national support body, the Association of Community Health Councils for England and Wales, was set up in 1977 (and there are similar bodies in Scotland and Northern Ireland).

The precise functions of CHCs have always been somewhat vague. They have no formal decision-making powers, and their sole statutory duties are to publish an annual report and to hold at least one annual meeting with the relevant district health authority. According to the Act by which they were established, each CHC has a duty 'to represent the interests in the health service of the public in its district',[1] and most CHCs have viewed their role as one of learning about local health concerns and assessing the services provided accordingly. In this regard, CHCs have produced a wide range of documents on local services, commenting on their effectiveness and making recommendations for change. Some have set up sub-committees to give deeper consideration to certain problems. In addition, they have played a part in furthering health education, attempting to promote public understanding of health issues, for instance by publishing leaflets on specific subjects. Finally, they have offered members of the public information and advice, often concerning specific problems or complaints procedures. Some hold 'surgeries' for this purpose.

Although CHCs have no formal powers, they do have certain rights. They have the right to ask for and receive information from health administrators and to visit and inspect those NHS premises controlled by health authorities (i.e. not doctors' surgeries). They have the right to be consulted about plans and to make representations to the district health authority. No hospital can be closed, or its use substantially changed, without prior consultation with the relevant CHC. Furthermore, each CHC has the right to send one member to meetings of the relevant district health authority, who can speak but not vote on issues under discussion. Some CHCs have also negotiated arrangements to attend meetings of other health bodies, such as health care planning teams, joint consultative committees and family practitioner committees, but their presence is solely discretionary.

The establishment of the CHCs did not derive from any manifest consumer pressure, but rather from a political commitment to give consumers some voice in an otherwise highly centralised and professionally dominated health system. The basic thrust of the NHS reorganisation in 1974 had been towards centralisation, with the health authority members accountable upwards and not representative of any particular political or professional constituencies. As a result, there was no means of ensuring the health consumer any voice in the new system. The invention of the community health councils provided one solution to a perceived need to provide such a mechanism; their functions may have been vague, but they served a clear political purpose.[2]

The role of the CHCs has remained a perennial subject for debate. Even before they were set up, Shirley Williams described them as 'the strangest bunch of administrative eunuchs any department had yet foisted on the House, a seraglio of useless and emasculated bodies.'[3] Admittedly, some changes did follow which altered their resources. Their functions were re-considered in 1974, with the publication of *Democracy in the NHS*, but few changes actually implemented. In 1979, the Report of the Royal Commission on the NHS reviewed the entire administration of the health service, and put forward various recommendations for strengthening the position of the CHCs.[4] Although the subsequent consultative document raised the possibility of disbanding them,[5] it was decided to retain the CHCs for the foreseeable future under the re-structured NHS.[6]

This discussion of the CHCs has been included here as they are generally looked upon as the principal means of effecting consumer participation in the health service. In fact, they do not really provide a forum for direct consumer participation at all. This is not only because they are not comprised strictly of consumers, but also because they do not entail in themselves the interaction of members with health service policy-makers. They are, instead, a kind of officially established pressure group, helping to mobilise consumer opinion and transmit it to those responsible for health administration. Where CHC members come into contact with policy-makers, in attending district health authority meetings or through informal discussions between them, direct participation can be seen to take place. But in the course of their everyday work, CHCs should be viewed as mechanisms facilitating indirect participation in health service administration, along with many other non-statutory consumer groups.

Patient participation groups (PPGs), in contrast, are systems for direct consumer participation in health administration. They have no statutory status, but represent an entirely voluntary response to a concern for greater contact between local surgeries and their patients. The first three were established by local doctors in three separate areas quite independently of one another in 1972-3, and the idea spread to other areas fairly rapidly. None the less, there remain very few of them in relation to the number of practices. By May 1981, there were thirty-two such groups operating in various locations throughout England and Wales.[7] In 1978, the National Association for Patient Participation in General Practice was established, to foster and support these developments.

Being voluntary bodies, there is no set structure for PPGs, but some common patterns can be noted. Most have been initiated by doctors, not patients, and have been set up around an individual practice or, more commonly, a health centre. Systems for selecting members vary; some elect members at public meetings, some circularise patients for nominations, and some have their members chosen by existing community groups. Although the officers of PPGs are typically chosen from the patient members, both doctors and other staff generally attend their meetings. In some cases, staff form a certain proportion of the formal membership. Most hold monthly meetings.

The functions of PPGs tend to revolve around the provision of feedback from patients about services received and the fostering of greater public education about health issues. They have made suggestions about existing arrangements, such as clinic opening hours, and proposed new ways in which patients might be helped, for instance organising transport to surgeries. They have led to the mobilisation of more voluntary activity among and on behalf of patients, both on an individual basis, such as baby-sitting and the collection of prescriptions, and on a group basis through the formation of new self-help groups. Some groups have established sub-committees to give special attention to particular categories of patients, such as the elderly, or specific health problems. They have also arranged public lectures to improve local health education, and some have also produced written material for the same purpose. Most groups have developed close links with their local community health council, exchanging both information and support, and in some cases having overlapping membership. Many have also proved to be active fund-raisers to support the new activities advocated.

As noted above, most patient participation groups were founded by doctors. Research on the motivations of the instigators suggests that there were a number of factors at work. While some felt that the development of these committees might pre-empt greater pressure on them from consumers, most were concerned to use the group to improve the service they provided. Some saw them as a means of furthering health education and increasing preventive care; others saw them as one vehicle for achieving a more responsive service, believing that general practitioners should be accountable to their patients.[8] They have not proved very controversial bodies, but the extent to which they are provided in those areas where they are most needed has been questioned. As the Royal Commission on the NHS stated, these groups have been set up 'by highly motivated doctors and seldom in practices where there is a real need for developing a dialogue between doctors and patients'.[9]

Housing

The roughly 6 million households who currently live in council housing in Britain have as their landlords those local authorities with housing responsibilities: the metropolitan and non-metropolitan district councils, the London boroughs and the Greater London Council. The organisation of housing management typically follows the traditional pattern of most local authority services. Although the supreme policy-making body is the local council, most housing management decisions are taken by the relevant committee, generally either a housing committee or a housing management committee. In many authorities, these committees have in turn set up sub-committees for specific management functions. Alongside the elected members of these committees, of course, there are a number of officers concerned with housing management, typically — but not universally — grouped within a housing department. On the tenants' side, many council tenants have joined together into tenants' associations, which act both as social organisations and as pressure groups on behalf of tenants. A national federation of these associations, the National Tenants' Organisation, was formed in 1977.

The participation of council tenants in the management of their housing became a statutory requirement under provisions in the 1980 Housing Act. It required all local authorities to set up arrangements for those tenants who would be 'substantially affected' by a management matter, to enable them both to be informed about proposals and to make their views known to the council. No decision on such matters may be taken before any such representations are considered.[10] The Act did not specify any single form of participation, however, which was left to local discretion.

The provisions of this Act did not come into effect until 1981, so at the time of writing the experience of local authorities with respect to them is relatively new. Many councils had, however, established arrangements for tenant participation prior to this time. Interest in the idea was particularly strong in the early 1970s and many existing schemes stem from this period. The most common system is a consultative committee, involving tenants and councillors. Some authorities, however, involve tenants directly on their housing committee or a management sub-committee. In some cases, there is a single authority-wide committee; in others, decentralised arrangements have been set up on a district or estate basis. Local councillors are almost always involved in these schemes, and most have housing officers in attendance. Tenant representatives are typically selected by individual tenant associations, but a few authorities have devised arrangements for their election.

Most tenant participation schemes provide tenants with only advisory powers, involving tenants either on consultative bodies or on council committees but without full membership status. In some cases, however, tenants have been given full voting powers as members of the housing committee or a housing sub-committee. Although tenant membership of the former is restricted by law to one-third of the total, there is no limit on the proportion of tenant members on a sub-committee, even where it has executive powers.[11]

The actual functions of tenant participation schemes vary considerably. Some operate as *de facto* complaint forums, in which tenants raise specific problems concerning housing maintenance and other local management issues. Others involve regular discussion of broader issues, such as estate modernisation plans or proposed changes in administrative procedures. Some explicitly preclude consideration of any financial issues, such as rents, but others enable these matters to be discussed along with any other issues tenants wish to raise.

On the whole, the impetus for establishing these arrangements did not derive from council tenants. Although tenant associations were proliferating in the 1970s, and some pressed their authorities for opportunities to participate, most of the schemes set up at that time were instigated by councillors or housing officers.[12] A great deal of interest had been generated in the idea among housing management professionals, and they set about finding ways of implementing it. Many schemes were established by local authorities, in fact, quite independently, with each having no knowledge of what the other was doing. Furthermore, its inclusion in the 1980 Housing Act, while supported by the National Tenants Organisation, was not obviously the result of tenant pressure. The idea of tenant participation had not only gained a certain political momentum at that time, but it was also seen by officials at the Department of the Environment as a means of reducing management problems on housing estates, such as vandalism. Its housing policy 'green paper', issued in 1977, had favoured the implementation of tenant participation,[13] and in the same year it published a handbook for local authorities on how to set up and run such schemes.[14] The idea of devolving management responsibility entirely to tenants, through the establishment of housing co-operatives, was also seriously explored at that time.[15]

Education

The provision of education to all children aged 5 to 16 is a statutory responsibility, and the vast majority of children in this age range attend state, or 'maintained', schools. While the Secretary of State for Education has overall responsibility for national educational policy, educational provision rests with the local education authorities. These are the county councils, the metropolitan district councils, the outer London borough councils and one authority for inner London. They provide primary schools, secondary schools, special schools for the handicapped, and may provide nursery schools and further education. Each education authority is required by law to have an education committee, composed of both councillors and co-opted members with 'educational expertise'. Typically, there are also a number of sub-committees concerned with specific subject areas. Each authority must also appoint a chief education officer, and as in the case of housing, there are additionally a number of officers concerned with educational administration, generally grouped within an education department. Individual schools or sets of schools are managed by boards of governors (formerly called 'boards of managers' in primary schools). These are composed of a minimum of three people, plus *ex officio* the school head, selected by the local education authority. They are expected to oversee the conduct and curriculum of the school.

The participation of parents as members of school governing boards became mandatory for new schools under the 1980 Education Act, but the compliance of existing schools with these provisions remained volun-tary. The possibility of making participation compulsory for existing schools at some future date was raised, however, in subsequent debate.[16] The Act required that each managing board include at least two parents of children at that school (or one in the case of 'aided' voluntary schools), to be elected by secret ballot by the parents as a whole.[17]

These provisions can be traced directly to recommendations made in 1977 by the Taylor Committee, set up to consider the composition and functions of school governing bodies, although the idea and practice of parent governors pre-dated its establishment. Its report proposed that each governing board should be composed of equal numbers of repre-sentatives of four groups: the local education authority, school staff, parents and the local community.[18] It also proposed that these bodies should be delegated greater powers, in terms of the issues about which they would be consulted, by local education authorities, although they would not have the ultimate responsibility for decision-making.

One interesting issue raised by the Taylor Committee was the potential role of pupils as school governors. It considered parental participation to be a necessary proxy for the involvement of children, the actual consumers of education. The Department of Education and Science had argued in its evidence to the committee that only persons aged 18 or over could hold public office, thereby excluding pupils from participation in governing boards. The Taylor Committee none the less proposed that secondary-school pupils should be allowed to participate as observers or, if the law were changed, as full members. As observers, they could receive papers, attend meetings and take part in discussions, but not vote. If they were to become full members, they would replace parent members.

Parents were never expressly debarred from membership of governing bodies, and interest in securing their involvement grew during the 1960s and 1970s. The Plowden Committee had recommended that parents be represented on the managing boards of primary schools in 1967.[19] By the time the Taylor Committee reported, the great majority of authorities had implemented parental representation on the governing boards of at least some of their schools. A survey noted in the Report indicated that by 1975 85 per cent of the authorities included some parents on their governing bodies and a few schools had implemented pupil participation as well.[20] By 1979, a new survey found that 90 per cent of authorities had some parental representation and 30 per cent had some participation by pupils, although often not with full powers. The majority of most governing boards, however, were appointed by the authority.[21] Although data are not readily available, some authorities have also co-opted parents on to their education committee, as persons with 'educational expertise'.

Unlike participation in the areas discussed above, the development of parental participation in education appears to derive more clearly from consumer pressure. During the 1960s, a number of organisations had been formed concerned with educational provision, and although their general aims were diverse, most were keen to extend opportunities for parental participation. It has been suggested that the growth of consumer interest in this idea arose from middle-class parents who were becoming increasingly reliant on the publicly provided system for educating their children.[22] One researcher ascribes their interest to the growing belief that educational standards were falling, a proposition that was receiving considerable publicity at the time. In addition, the economic recession fuelled their concern, as they became increasingly worried that their aspirations for their children might not be fulfilled.[23] Finally, parental interest in participation was partly a response to the growing pressures from teachers to increase *their* influence over schools, which had been eroded by the growth of educational administrators in the enlarged education authorities.[24] Although the 1980 legislation could be seen to derive from recommendations of the Taylor Committee, the establishment of that Committee was itself partly a response to demands from parents' groups.

The personal social services

Unlike the other subject areas discussed here, the personal social services do not have an easily identifiable common function. Comprising those activities carried out by local authority social services departments, these services are linked only by their administrative base and their focus on providing social care to people with special needs. They include the provision of residential accommodation for the elderly, infirm and children in care, certain direct services such as day nurseries and home helps, and miscellaneous other activities such as monitoring services available for the disabled and carrying out adoptions. These services were given a single administrative link following the review of social service needs carried out by Lord Seebohm in 1968. They are the responsibility of the county councils, metropolitan district councils and the London boroughs. These authorities are required by law to have a social services committee and a director of social services responsible to it. Many have set up sub-committees to consider particular problems. As with all local government services, there are a number of officers responsible for administering the personal social services, typically grouped within a social services department. These are generally organised into area teams.

The idea of consumer participation in the provision of the personal social services was first given serious expression in the Seebohm Report. It was concerned to foster general public interest in the social services, viewing them as 'directed to the well-being of the whole of the community and not only of social casualties'.[25] As part of this approach, it recommended both individual and group participation in the provision and planning of services. One suggestion it put forward was for the establishment of advisory bodies, to be centred on the area offices of social services departments. These would be composed of local councillors and consumers and would discuss the services provided. It also suggested that consumers might be involved directly in the Social Services Committee, or a sub-committee on an area basis.

These proposals do not appear to have been widely implemented, although there is only limited information available on current practices. Some authorities have set up consultative committees or sub-committees of their social services committee on an authority-wide or area basis with the intention of bringing the clients' perspective into policy-making. These do not generally involve clients directly, however, but involve instead representatives of various voluntary groups concerned with their welfare, often centred on specific categories such as the elderly or handicapped. Such spokesmen have also been co-opted on to some local authority social services committees. One visible form of direct consumer participation in this area is the involvement of residents in the management of some old people's residential homes and, similarly, of users in the management of some day-care centres. This, again, appears to be uncommon, but where it exists can vary from participation in service provision (meal preparation or maintenance work) to participation in committees to deal with complaints or even determine policy. Experiments in 'patch systems' also entail participation of clients, as well as the community, in service provision.[26]

Social security

The fifth component of the various 'services' which comprise traditional social policy is the general area of cash benefits or social security. Excluding those arrangements by which individuals gain only a limited financial assistance from the state, such as child benefits, it strictly includes only those payments which provide the principal or sole source of income to the recipient. The major cash benefits comprise both contributory benefits, such as unemployment insurance and retirement pensions and the means-tested supplementary benefits scheme. These benefits are administered by the Department of Health and Social Security on a decentralised basis through local offices. A lay committee, the Social Security Advisory Committee (SSAC) advises the DHSS on both its insurance and supplementary benefits scheme, replacing the former Supplementary Benefits Commission (SBC) and two other advisory committees.

There has been relatively little discussion about the potential for 'consumer' or claimant participation in the administration of these various benefits schemes. The sole area in which it has been seriously mooted is, perhaps surprisingly, the administration of supplementary benefits. In 1977, the National Consumer Council urged the Supplementary Benefits Commission to introduce local committees, including claimants, to discuss local problems and generally monitor the administration of the supplementary benefits scheme.[27] In response, the DHSS commissioned a short study to consider the feasibility of this proposal and to make recommendations about how it might be implemented.

The report on this project recommended that two experimental groups, composed of claimants, staff and representatives of some local organisations, should be established and monitored over a two-year period.[28] The 'user' membership was widened to include claimants of both contributory and supplementary benefits. It was suggested that these groups might improve the information available locally about benefits, discuss local administrative issues inasmuch as these affect claimants, and feed up to headquarters ideas about the operation of the scheme at local level. These committees would have no formal powers, but would facilitate discussion of issues and might result in useful suggestions. Although these recommendations were agreed by the DHSS, and had the enthusiastic support of the SBC itself, they were never implemented due to lack of co-operation from the civil service staff unions. The idea has not arisen since on any political agenda.

Environmental planning

Although the activity of environmental planning is not typically linked with social policy, its exclusion from a discussion of the contexts of participation would seem inappropriate. Planning can refer to a wide range of activities, but it is commonly used to describe the development of two kinds of plans by local authorities. Structure plans outline general policy for the development of an area, concentrating particularly on such issues as housing, transport and industrial policies. They are drawn up by county councils, and must be submitted to the Secretary of State for approval. Local plans, providing detailed proposals for land use in a smaller area, must be devised in conformity with the strategic structure plan. They are drawn up by district councils (and London boroughs) and do not need to be submitted for approval. In fact, while the development of structure plans has been proceeding steadily, local planning has not kept pace, and relatively few local plans have been adopted.[29] Within each local authority, there is typically a Planning Committee (or similar body with a different name) and a Planning Department responsible to it.

Planners must enable members of the public to take part in the planning process under provisions introduced in the Town and Country Planning Act of 1968 and consolidated in 1971. Planning authorities are required, with respect to both structure and local plans, to inform those expected to want to make recommendations that they can do so and to give them six weeks in which to make their views known.[30] When the structure plan is submitted to the Secretary of State, the authority must also submit a statement showing what it has done to effect public participation, and the plan may be rejected if he is not satisfied that sufficient efforts have been made in this direction. Authorities must similarly inform the Secretary of State about steps they have taken for public participation with respect to local plans.

The 1968 Act did not set out any single method by which public participation should be implemented, but the Skeffington Committee was set up to consider this issue. Its report, *People and Planning*, was published in 1969, and stressed the importance of providing information about plans to local people affected by them.[31] In addition to a number of suggestions for publicising planning proposals, such as exhibitions and films, it recommended the establishment of local community forums to enable groups to discuss plans with authority planners. Co-option of representatives of community groups on to planning committees was also considered, but thought to be too limited in terms of the numbers involved. Expressing particular concern over the problem of the non-joiners, the Committee also recommended the appointment of community development officers to mobilise interest in local groups.

None of these proposals has been statutorily required of local authorities, and advice on this issue from the Department of the Environment has been somewhat vague. Certainly, neither the idea of community forums nor that of community development officers received enthusiastic endorsement. Local authorities have tried even so, in keeping with the requirements on them, both to publicise their plans and to gauge public reaction. They have prepared and distributed material about their plans, from sophisticated reports to local news-sheets; they have carried out surveys to canvas local opinion, both casually at exhibitions and systematically through survey research agencies. Finally, and the only technique involving direct participation, they have set up both public meetings to discuss plans with anyone wishing to attend and more private consultations with representatives of active community groups.

But all of these activities concern only the initial stages of the planning process, and there are in addition methods by which the public can be involved subsequently. First, when a structure plan is submitted to the Secretary of State, it must again be publicised and the public informed that they can make objections directly to him. If he considers it appropriate, he can set up an 'examination in public' (often referred to as an EIP), at which both the planning authority and objectors may discuss certain issues before a given panel. While the decision to set up an EIP at all, the appointment of the panel and its chairman, and the designation of the issues which may be discussed are all left to the discretion of the Secretary of State, this procedure does allow some measure of direct public participation in the later stages of the planning process. There is no requirement, however, that a report be issued, nor that any recommendations arising from the examination be accepted. Furthermore, there is no automatic right for members of the public to be heard.[32]

This procedure does not operate in the case of local plans, but the district council can convene a 'public enquiry' at a similar stage in the planning process. There are fewer restrictions on these, and any evidence can be submitted to them. They are attended by a member of the planning inspectorate, who must 'hear' objections and produce a report, and the council is expected to take some account of his recommendations. Again, this system provides an additional opportunity for ensuring some public participation in the later stages of the planning process.

The idea of encouraging greater public participation in planning developed in the mid-1960s, fuelled by pressures both from within and from outside the planning profession. It has been argued that the planners were primarily concerned to re-define the nature of their task, making it more comprehensive but also more clearly delineated, and sought to increase public receptivity to their work through participation.[33] Critics of the profession included both local community and action groups, concerned to achieve specific objectives, and more general commentators, concerned to widen the opportunities for public questioning of what had previously been seen as solely technical issues. While the implementation of the 1968 Act may have been expected to satisfy both sets of groups, the publication of the Skeffington Report and subsequent debate over both political and technical questions only served to heighten tensions between them. During the 1970s, however, interest in public participation in planning slowly abated, revived only occasionally by publication of academic or professional reports on the subject.

Public employees

Finally, what about the workers? With all these developments in the
opportunities available for consumers to participate in social policy
decision-making, it would be surprising if the cause of workers lay
entirely dormant. And, indeed, the 1970s witnessed a heightened
interest in the general subject of employee participation, culminating
in the publication of the Bullock Report on industrial democracy.[34]
While this focussed on the private sector, it had some impact on discussions about the public sector as well. The current social policy scene
includes some examples of employee participation in practice, to which
some very brief attention is given here. Most of these involve professional groups, however, rather than para-professionals or manual
workers.

The two areas in which professional groups have acquired an established role in the decision-making process are health and education.
With respect to the former, the medical professions, particularly
doctors, have been given various forms of representation in the policy-
making process for many years. (Strictly speaking, it should be added,
general practitioners are not 'employees' of the NHS, but they can be
so viewed for purposes of this analysis.) As noted above, both the
regional health authorities and the district health authorities include
staff representatives; the RHAs, in addition, include a number of
medical professionals as members, appointed in a personal capacity.
Furthermore, one hospital specialist and one general practitioner,
chosen by their professional groups, are members of each district
management team. Finally, there are many advisory bodies representing various professional groups at all levels of NHS administration.
There can be no question that the medical professions, although not
para-medical staff, are well represented in the NHS decision-making
process.

With respect to teachers, they too have a number of ways of getting
their voice heard in the administration of education. They are the one
group of council employees who are not explicitly debarred from
membership of local authority committees in the council by whom
they are employed. They have frequently been co-opted on to the
education committee as persons with 'educational expertise', and can
be found as co-opted members of sub-committees as well. Places on the
former are typically allocated in proportion to local membership of the
main teachers' unions. Furthermore, the 1980 Education Act required

that at least one or two teachers, depending on the size of the school, be made members of the governing boards of new schools, along with parents, again following recommendations of the Taylor Committee. As previous guidance to local education authorities had expressly recommended their exclusion from these boards, this represented a substantial policy change. Some authorities had, however, involved teachers from other schools on their governing bodies in order to give some representation to teaching interests. Again, ancillary workers have had little involvement in school administration, although the Taylor Committee Report did recommend that they be given a more substantial role.

In all other areas of social policy provision, the participation of workers has proved only an occasional development. In the case of housing, local authority manual workers' unions have argued that they be given some representation, along with tenants, on participation committees in order to be able to respond to any criticisms levelled against them. Instances of their involvement are, however, relatively rare. Efforts to involve employees in the decision-making of social services departments can also be found in some authorities.[35] Arguments that local authority employees should be represented on council committees, or even the full council itself, have been put forward from time to time as parallel arrangements to workers being given seats on the board of private companies.[36] Such proposals would require a change in the law, however, and have not generally met with much enthusiasm.

Summary and discussion

This chapter has outlined the major arrangements which have been established for consumer and employee participation in those services typically of interest to students of social policy. It must be reiterated, however, that there are many other contexts which have been omitted from this discussion. In the field of education, for instance, student participation in university decision-making received considerable attention in the early 1970s, and many local arrangements were devised to effect it. Consumer participation in the nationalised industries, involving some of the most long-standing systems for consumer representation, has similarly been the subject of some interest from time to time. The various consultative committees set up around the fuel boards, transport systems and the post office could all have been included here. Similarly, new arrangements for employee participation in some nationalised industries, devised during the last decade, could equally be mentioned. It has simply seemed easier to limit the material presented.

But among the diverse arrangements for participation covered in this discussion, what common patterns can be noted? First, with respect to *who* has been invited to participate, by far the greatest attention has been paid to those directly affected by policy decisions, the consumers. Despite occasional nods in the direction of the broader public (the 'general community'), as in the Taylor Report on school governing boards or the Seebohm Report on the personal social services, most practical proposals have focussed on the direct service consumers. Furthermore, there has been relatively little movement in the direction of implementing employee participation in this area. It is only the more powerful professional groups, such as doctors and teachers, who have managed to gain a regular voice in the decision-making process.

Secondly, with respect to whom the participants participate *with*, this varies, not surprisingly, with the locus of participation. In the case of services provided by local authorities, some schemes entail participation in council committees or sub-committees, necessitating involvement with councillors, although with officers in attendance. Other schemes entail participation at the point of service delivery, such as school governing boards, in which case those with whom the participants are involved vary according to the pre-existing arrangements for decision-making. Senior staff, such as the school head, may be particularly prominent here. Outside the local authority sphere, similar considerations pertain. Whereas community health councils have greatest contact with members of the health authorities and management teams, for instance, members of patients' participation groups are primarily involved with local doctors. It may be noted that services also vary in the relative interest taken by officers or elected members in participation arrangements; planners have traditionally been more involved than councillors in participation in planning, whereas councillors have often taken a greater interest than officers in tenant participation schemes.

Thirdly, with respect to the powers ascribed to the new participants, these are generally fairly limited. Virtually all bodies established for the express purpose of introducing participation have only an advisory or consultative status; they cannot take binding decisions. Even where, in contrast, the participants are involved in an existing body, such as a local authority education committee or housing sub-committee, they frequently do not have full membership status. In a number of cases, the participants are enabled to speak but not vote. Furthermore, they are rarely more than a small minority of the total membership. By law, co-opted (non-elected) members of a council committee cannot comprise more than one-third of its members; this provision does not apply, however, to sub-committees even where they have been delegated executive powers.

Fourthly, while the selection procedures vary considerably, they frequently involve intermediate bodies between the general consumer (or employee) population and the statutory authority. In the case of workers, these are, of course, the relevant unions; in the case of consumers, they are whatever associations exist who can speak for the relevant groups: parents' associations, community associations and so forth. Where these have not existed, authorities have often tried to foster their development, both by using various community work techniques and by simply declaring all relevant consumers, such as parents at a given school, to be members of a new association.

Finally, without trespassing on the territory of subsequent chapters, concerned with the broader issues raised by the introduction of participation, it may be useful to draw attention to a few common problems arising from the specific structures outlined here. A great deal of concern is regularly expressed about the extent to which the participants may be said to be representative of the larger consumer (or worker) population. Given the common reliance on intermediate bodies for selecting the participants, this concern is hardly surprising; those who either have no association to belong to or choose not to belong to their relevant group are effectively disenfranchised. Efforts to foster the formation of new groups, and to encourage non-joiners to become involved, represent attempts to minimise this problem, but it is unlikely ever to be fully solved. Nor is the establishment of a more open election system necessarily any fairer, since it must rely on some system for publicising its existence and this may not reach all members of the relevant population. Participation arrangements centred on a single institution which is easily in touch with all of its consumers, such as a school or residential home, can most easily overcome this problem. A local surgery, in contrast, has no inexpensive means of publicising a participation group to all of its users, since most of the latter do not attend it on a regular basis.

A related problem, focussed not on the machinery for selecting the participants but on its effects, is the potentially limited dialogue between the wider body of consumers and their representatives. If the latter are supposed to speak for the concerns of the former, by what means can anyone be certain that they do so accurately? Furthermore, to the extent that participation is seen as a vehicle for transmitting information *to* consumers, by what means and to whom do the representatives report back? These problems are eased where there are consumer groups, such as tenants' associations, with whom the representatives can discuss issues raised, although the issue of the non-joiner remains. Where there are no such associations, as in the case of users of a local surgery, they are not readily surmounted.

A third problem, arising wherever participation arrangements are not statutorily required, is the uneven distribution of opportunities to participate. Instead of inequities between consumers within a given authority, as raised above, differential implementation of participation gives rise to inequities between consumers of different authorities. Parents in some schools, but not others, can take part in governing boards; patients in some surgeries, but not others, can make their views known to doctors, and so forth. Furthermore, it is often suggested that such schemes tend to be set up exactly where they are least needed, that is where decision-makers are already responsive to the views of their consumers. As long as the introduction of participation is left to local discretion, however, there is little that can be done to overcome this problem.

Finally, on a much more pragmatic level, there are a host of issues which are regularly raised by those concerned to ensure that participation functions most effectively. This is not a manual on how to set up participation schemes, and these issues need not be resolved here, but a few of the more major ones may be usefully noted.[37] With respect to the participants, there is a regular dilemma about numbers; more consumers may express more points of view, but a limited number of consumer representatives may prove more effective spokesmen. The selection procedure, as noted above, also causes problems; consumer associations may be an efficient mechanism but not clearly representative, while elections may prove cumbersome and not necessarily any fairer to everyone. With respect to the decision-makers with whom the participants become involved, there are again regular problems. Those in senior positions, whether elected or appointed, may be thought the most crucial, but may also prove to be the least frequent attenders because of other commitments.

Nor is there any greater consensus on questions of the appropriate structure or functions of participation arrangements. Decentralised or highly local schemes may concentrate on what the consumers know best, but are expensive to run everywhere and may be thought ultimately entirely powerless. Participation in existing committees may be easily arranged and give consumers access to the 'real' decision-makers, but may not prove an effective forum for airing consumers' problems because of pressures of other business. Similarly, providing consumers full voting rights on such committees may appear to give them the greatest voice, but because of the limited numbers involved this may eventually be less effective than participation in other forums. In many policy issues there is also a problem of the timing of participation, the stage in the decision-making process at which consumers should be brought in. Consumers may be unable to specify or relate to abstract goals or very broad problems, but may also be unable to sway opinion on detailed proposals once these have been worked on and priorities established.

Such issues are, if not endless, certainly manifold. They are the practical headaches which anyone charged with devising participation arrangements or improving existing ones must face. This discussion has not only done little justice to their complexity but also has touched on only a few. Furthermore, it should be remembered that formal schemes for direct participation, as described in this chapter, represent only one part of what can be done to get people involved. There are also informal arrangements for direct participation, such as public meetings or small discussion sessions, and a range of mechanisms for indirect participation, such as social surveys or involvement in consumers' associations. Needless to say, there are advantages and disadvantages in fostering participation by any of these means, but these and other practical questions must be pursued elsewhere. Attention must be drawn to deeper issues.

4 The claims for participation

Underlying discussion on virtually all policy issues is the crucial question: Is the policy desirable? Should it be implemented and, if so, why? It is often thought that the answer is simply a matter of values or goals, of knowing in effect whose side one is on. But in many cases there is, in fact, a prior problem — establishing what the consequences of the policy actually are. For until it is clear what impact it has, whose interests it serves, no decision can be sensibly taken — whatever one's ideological persuasion — about whether the policy is desirable.

So it is in the case of participation. It is well known that it has been advocated by people with many different viewpoints for many different reasons. To some extent this diversity is due to attention to different sorts of considerations. Some are primarily interested in the effects of participation on the individuals involved, for instance, while others are concerned about its impact on the decisions they take. This in itself presents no particular problem. But in addition, some of its advocates and opponents base their position on conflicting diagnoses of the direction of its impact. Some believe that through participation consumers' influence over decisions will be increased, for example, whereas others assert the reverse will be the case. On a somewhat different plane, some believe that participation will make the participants more accepting of existing social norms, whereas others, again, assert the reverse will be the case. The presence of such contrasting expectations not only creates some strange bedfellows but presents the student of participation a puzzling analytical problem. Who is correct? And how did they reach such divergent conclusions?

This chapter sets out the claims which have been made both for and against participation, the reasons offered for introducing it and for opposing its introduction. While focussed primarily on its assumed effects, that is what people claim it will do, it is impossible to avoid some discussion of values, that is why people claim it is (or is not) desirable. The following chapter subjects these claims to critical examination, developing a general analysis of what participation means in practice. Through a consideration of the processes set in motion by its introduction, a means of both understanding and reconciling the conflicting diagnoses is suggested.

First, a short comment on contexts is in order. As demonstrated in the preceding chapter, participation has been implemented in many different policy areas, and one might expect to find little comparability in the grounds on which it has been advocated from one context to another. Similarly, different arguments might be expected with regard to the participation of workers, compared with that of consumers, and with regard to participation in decision-making, compared with that in service delivery. Happily, these expectations are unfounded. Despite the varied circumstances in which participation can occur, there is considerable congruence in the claims put forward for (and against) its introduction. This consistency is very helpful here, for it enables the subject to be explored as a whole. The arguments can be presented systematically in terms of general themes, rather than focussing on individual contexts in turn. The following discussion is generally phrased in terms of the participation of consumers in decision-making, however, in order to focus attention on the analytical, rather than the contextual, issues. Illustrative quotations are drawn from a variety of policy areas.

All arguments for or against participation focus on one or both of two distinct, although frequently muddled, issues. These concern the *process* of participation on the one hand, and the *substantive consequences* to which this process gives rise on the other. This distinction, of course, is not unique to the study of participation; it arises wherever there are processes of human interaction which can lead to varied results. In reviewing the major grounds for political justification, Dworkin makes a similar distinction between what he calls 'arguments of principle' and 'arguments of policy'. As he writes:

Arguments of principle justify a political decision by showing that the decision respects or secures some individual or group right. . . . Arguments of policy justify a political decision by showing that the decision advances or protects some collective goal of the community as a whole.[1]

To clarify this distinction further, one illustration may prove helpful. Democracy can be advocated on the basis either that it is the fairest system of government or that it leads to the most desirable policies. While many would argue that it is best on both counts, this begs the question of their position when a conflict arises between them. Where a policy position is particularly strongly held, for instance, it may be argued that it should prevail even where it would be 'undemocratic' to allow it to do so. Conversely, it may be argued that a particularly offensive policy should be implemented because it was democratically agreed. In both situations, it can be seen that there is a clear conflict of values which is not comfortably resolved. In the same way, the case for participation as a means of establishing due process is independent of the case for it in terms of specific policy results; arguments on the basis of the former should be divorced from any considerations about the resulting effects.

Participation and due process

The case for participation on grounds of due process stresses the overriding importance of consumers' rights. It is argued that those who will be affected by decisions have a basic right to have some influence over their outcome, and therefore should be brought into the decision-making process in some capacity. In the words of the legal maxim, what touches all should be approved by all (*quod omnes tangit, ab omnibus approbatur est*). Individual consumers should be the judge of their own interests; whether or not they are capable of making a constructive contribution to any policy debate, the debate itself can only be judged equitable if they are involved.

This argument is normally asserted as a self-evident proposition based on the situation of the people to be involved. With respect to planning, for example, one prominent politician is quoted as declaring, 'I accept . . . a planning process in which the individual citizen, whether alone or acting in a pressure group, has a fundamental right to influence the direction taken in the area in which he lives.'[2] Occasionally, however, an attempt is made to provide some underlying justification. An advocate of employee participation in the administration of social services states: 'The citizen's "investment" in a modern democratic society accords him the right to take part in the wider political process; the argument for worker participation could be considered a logical extension of this.'[3] More cautiously, participation is sometimes asserted as a right only under certain specified circumstances. Julia Parker links this with rights of citizenship, but suggests some boundaries:

> The kind of equality of status implied in the idea of citizenship
> carries with it the right to take part in the planning of services
> which vitally affect people's lives and in decisions which do not call
> for some kind of professional or expert knowledge not possessed by
> the layman.[4]

It may be noted that conflicts can arise in determining *which* consumers have a right to participation, as well as between the rights of consumers and those of employees of a given service. In the case of education, for example, there is some potential conflict between parents and their older children, and between both groups and teachers, in any claim to a right to participate in school management decisions. This problem can prove the source of mild embarrassment to those asserting consumers' rights, where they do not wish to appear to be limiting those of anyone else. Of course, exclusivity of rights need not be claimed.

The case against participation on grounds of process simply reverses the group to which priority should be given. Instead of placing primary emphasis on the rights of those directly affected by decisions, it suggests that those who must bear the costs of these decisions should have the sole right to influence their outcome. While it is reasonable for decision-makers to take the interests of those they are affecting into account, the latter do not have any over-riding right to be involved in framing policy. Indeed, although they may be the beneficiaries of services, it may be questioned whether they should appropriately be termed the 'consumers':

> Students at university level often argue that they are the consumers
> and that they should therefore have the major say in academic
> decisions. . . . They fail to appreciate . . . that if this model is pressed
> home, it can be argued that the general public and beneficient
> business men are the real consumers, for they put up most of the
> money.[5]

Thus, some claim that the introduction of participatory measures, far from ensuring a more equitable decision-making process, actually makes it less fair by giving an undue advantage to certain groups over others. Consumer participation is deemed, in short, a retrogressive measure. As Friedrich writes, again in the context of student participation, their representatives have power 'without the restraint of effective responsibility' (because of their temporary status as students), and 'participation of this kind, far from being democratic in the tradition of Western constitutional democracy, is in fact a kind of privileging of special groups of persons, reminiscent of feudalism'.[6]

Participation and individual development

But most of the claims both for and against the introduction of participation do not concern its value as a process, but focus instead on the consequences to which it gives rise. Whatever the policy context in which they are introduced, arrangements for consumer participation are generally claimed to have two distinct types of effect. It is asserted that, on the one hand, they affect the direct well-being and behaviour of the participants while, on the other, they affect the decisions taken by or for this group. This distinction is not entirely straightforward in practice, since changed decisions may have significant effects for the well-being of the participants and vice versa, but it provides a useful basis on which to frame discussion. It has gained wide acceptance among writers on this subject, and the two contrasting effects are commonly labelled 'developmental' and 'instrumental' respectively. As Parry writes: ' "Developmental" theories see political participation as an essential part of the development of human capacities. "Instrumental" theories treat political participation as a means to some more restricted end such as the better defense of individual or group interests.'[7] In fact, both should be seen as instrumental, but concerned with achieving different sorts of results.

Considering first the developmental effects, participation clearly affects the people involved in many different ways, ranging from the immediate to the long-term. The introduction of participatory measures has consequently been advocated on a variety of developmental grounds; four distinct claims concern what participation will do for the direct participants. First, participation is seen as a way of ensuring those involved a sense of dignity and self-respect, which cannot be attained by any other means. It is argued that where decisions are made by others on their behalf, whatever the good intentions, consumers can have no sense of personal involvement in them. Participation in discussions about their everyday lives is therefore fundamentally important to individuals' self-fulfilment, as well as freedom:

> The social theory of democracy . . . argues that it is of the essence of a truly human life that certain decisions are made by the individual himself, not because they are better decisions . . . but because the 'control of decisions that affect a man's life' must be his before a man can be free.[8]

This can also be stated in the negative:

> Participation is . . . the active expression of our faith in the dignity and worth of the individual. To deny effective participation, including the opportunity to choose, to be heard, to discuss, to criticise, to protest and to challenge decisions regarding the most fundamental conditions of existence, is to deny the individual's own worth and to confirm his impotence and subservience.[9]

In the context of worker participation in management, this argument is commonly phrased in terms of job satisfaction. As one administrator in a social services department writes:

> There are staff at the base of our hierarchy who have considerable expertise and experience to contribute and who, by doing so, will gain greater job satisfaction, experience a reduction in powerlessness and an increase in self-respect and influence.[10]

The second claim for participation stresses the part it can play in the development of people's capacities. It is suggested that participation not only enhances the individual's ability to cope intelligently with a new range of issues but also increases his self-confidence to tackle problems in other spheres. Through discussion and consideration of varying types of issues, people are given a chance to learn about new problems and solutions to them; if they make a few mistakes, they will also learn from them. Participation is not only about making the participants more fulfilled; it is also about making them more fully developed human beings.

Some advocate participation on this basis as a useful training ground for related, but more demanding, activities, such as involvement in consumer or worker co-operatives. This was a frequent rationale for tenant participation schemes in the early 1970s, when enthusiasm for housing co-operatives was especially strong. The participation of certain types of professionals, such as social workers, in administrative decision-making has also been advocated to enhance their sensitivity to clients' own needs for involvement.[11] But others take a much broader view. The term 'efficacy' has been coined to refer to people's belief in their ability to influence the outcome of decisions, and it is claimed that participation leads to a heightened degree of efficacy with respect to many aspects of life. As Pateman writes:

> The major function of participation in the theory of participatory democracy is therefore an educative one, educative in the very widest sense, including both the psychological aspect and the gaining of practice in democratic skills and procedures. . . . Participation develops and fosters the very qualities necessary for it; the more individuals participate the better able they are to do so.[12]

The third argument can be seen as a very particular variant of the second, but sufficiently distinctive to require separate discussion. It suggests that participation is necessary for individuals to discover their own real interests, to learn not only about their environment and how to cope with it but also about themselves. This position is taken by Bachrach, who argues that participation, 'in making decisions that significantly affect him and his community . . . is an essential means for the individual to discover his real needs through the intervening discovery of himself as a social human being'.[13] Such participation is not simply a convenient route to achieve this end, it is the only one, he continues, as can be demonstrated in the negative for workers:

> Denied this right to participate, the worker has no basis upon which to form intelligent opinions, to articulate his interests, to gain insights that could well add positively to his work environment and give his life meaning as a contributing member of society.[14]

Finally, on a more limited perspective, participation is advocated for the 'expressive' benefits it provides for those involved. It is argued that ordinary people have few opportunities to express themselves with respect to policy issues in the course of their regular home and work routine, and arrangements for participation provide an obvious vehicle for this purpose. Put in everyday language, this proposes that participation is fun. None the less, a stirring case can be made on these grounds, as demonstrated by this statement of why people want to become involved:

> People demand to participate sometimes mainly, sometimes simply, because they want to be joked with, gossiped with, applauded, teased, argued with, reassured — in short, to count in the others' eyes as friends or possible friends, as team-mates, or as worthy rivals — perhaps as all three at once.[15]

In summary, four separate claims have been set out here with respect to the developmental impact of consumer participation on the individuals directly involved. Participation is seen as a means of achieving greater individual fulfilment, personal development, self-awareness and some immediate satisfaction. Few people wish to denigrate these ideals, and the case against participation is rarely stated with them as a central focus. Nor is it often suggested that participation is directly detrimental to human fulfilment or development. But the significance of participation for achieving these ends is sometimes questioned. As Peter Marcuse writes, with respect to tenant participation in housing management:

> Is it better to have many things wrong with one's housing, so one can maximise the involvement and exercise of control to change them? . . . Are decisions as to his housing among those, assuming there are such, which a man must make for himself to be free? Could not most decisions as to housing be seen as trivial from the lofty perspective of the fulfilment of the human being? Could people perhaps have better things to do with their time (or perhaps more important crises to face) than to get involved in the management of their housing?[16]

Some do claim, however, that the overall impact of participation on the development of consumers is detrimental to their longer-term interests. By focussing their energies and attention on themselves, participation deflects their potential concern for wider issues:

> Is the *sense* of community really enough? Is it enough to appease pangs of conscience, or make a beautiful or shocking gesture, or engage in meaningful personal relations, or have a moment in the

limelight, or enjoy the pleasure of self-expression, or have fun
while coming alive or shaking things up? Can these things be
enough — great as they are — if the structure of privilege and the
system of cruelty remain intact?[17]

But the case for participation on developmental grounds is often
taken one step further. In addition to the direct effects for the participants, the greater fulfilment and increased efficacy to which it is believed to lead, there are indirect effects for society at large which can be
traced to its introduction. By taking part in the processes of policy-
making, individuals are said to develop a heightened sense of social
integration. This means that they will not only ascribe greater legitimacy to their political institutions but also will prove more willing to
comply with them. It is suggested that 'opening up the agency decision-
making processes to public participation would tend among other
things to make agency decisions more acceptable to the public and thus
more likely to be enforceable.'[18]

Not surprisingly, this position has found particularly fertile ground
among those who are actively involved in maintaining existing institutions, who are often concerned to assure themselves that they have
public approval. Here, for example, are comments from a government
circular on public participation in planning:

> If the policies to be embodied in the plans are to be understood and
> generally accepted, and if the proposals in them are to be imple-
> mented successfully, the authorities must carry the public with
> them, by formulating, for public discussion, the aims and objectives
> of the policies and then the options for realising those aims and
> objectives.[19]

This position is often stated less baldly, however, in terms of encouraging citizens to appreciate a wider point of view. It was one of the key
bases for political participation envisaged by John Stuart Mill; such
involvement was, he wrote:

> the practical part of the political education of a free people, taking
> them out of the narrow circle of personal and family selfishness,
> and accustoming them to the comprehension of joint interests, the
> management of joint concerns — habituating them to act from
> public or semi-public motives, and guide their conduct by aims

which unite instead of isolating them from one another. Without these habits and powers, a free constitution can neither be worked nor preserved. . . .[20]

Some claim that one effect of such changed attitudes will be changed behaviour, and this in itself provides a justification for introducing participation, especially where it affects other people. Parental participation in schools, for example, is seen as a means of generating commitment to education generally; as one enthusiast argues, 'a greater sense of commitment by parents to the schools their children attend is also likely to increase the proportion who individually give education high priority at home.'[21] Tenant participation in housing management is similarly advocated as a means of increasing tenants' sense of responsibility for their estates so that various forms of anti-social behaviour are reduced. A housing manager asserts, 'the more a tenant is involved in a property, the more care and interest he will show, and there will be a spin-off in the reduction of vandalism.'[22]

Not everyone, however, considers these general effects to be desirable, and a case against participation is commonly posed on exactly these grounds. What it achieves, it is argued, should be termed not 'social integration' but 'social control', for it serves to maintain the existing social order. The legitimation of existing institutions may be welcomed by those who benefit from them, but it does little for those who seek change. The East London Claimants' Union, for instance, declares:

Any of this 'participation' would be a sell-out to the system and an attempt on the part of the establishment to absorb our militancy. To the establishment, participation merely means that a few of us will help 'them' to make decisions about us.[23]

Co-option can prove a powerful tool in the hands of those in authority, dampening the enthusiasm of the very people who are most needed to fight the consumer cause; as John Dearlove states:

[Participation] can force, or educate, the participants to gain an awareness of governmental problems and policies and this will not only inhibit the public from pressing for solutions to their own problems, but will also enable the authorities to legitimise their decisions with the stamp of public approval.[24]

It should, perhaps, be noted that while two very different stances on participation have been presented here, they do not differ in their analysis of what participation does. Both concur that its impact, for a variety of reasons, is to infuse those who are involved with a greater sense of commitment to the existing social system. This will affect not only their own personal behaviour but also their willingness to 'take on' the system in the interests of change. Participation is simply favoured or opposed in line with the value accorded to these ends.

But some do not accept this analysis. Participation does not tame the participant, it is argued, but quite the reverse; by becoming involved in deliberations about their services, consumers' enthusiasm for pressing for change is likely to increase. Participation can prove, in fact, a significant mechanism for catalysing public interest toward more general political mobilisation. This is the position of many community organisers, who welcome participation for this reason. Saul Alinsky, for instance, suggested that attempts to gain citizen control over specific local issues 'often constitute the subject matter for mounting campaigns, developing interests and providing an agenda for action, in order to attain the primary objective of organisation control'.[25] Others might equally strongly oppose participation in order to avoid such consequences, although such a position is rarely stated.

Participation and decisions on policy

But most of the interest in the idea of consumer participation, and most of the claims which have been made for or against its introduction, have been based not on its developmental effects but on its impact on policy. The introduction of consumers into the decision-making process is advocated or opposed on the grounds that they will affect the nature of the decisions stemming from it. These claims must now be examined.

The case for participation is often put with deceptive simplicity. It is necessary to involve consumers in discussions with service providers, it is said, both in order to increase mutual understanding and to achieve better services. Take these examples from planning (the Skeffington Report), education (the Taylor Report) and housing (a local government officer) respectively:

The objective is clear — to establish and maintain a better understanding between the public and the planning authority which will be of benefit to both.[26]

We believe that all parties concerned for a school's success — the local education authority, the staff, the parents and the local community — should be brought together so that they can discuss, debate and justify the proposals which any one of them may seek to implement.[27]

Our reorganisation [of local government] will be judged a success or failure according to whether or not it brings about an improvement in the service we give, and whether it brings about a closer link between those who make the decisions and those who bear the consequences.[28]

These statements appear reasonable enough on first glance. More discussion and debate should improve the decisions which emerge from it. But two very distinct claims for participation are in fact couched uncomfortably together within such broad assertions. The proponents of each have strongly differing views about what participation achieves. Furthermore, they agree neither on the nature of the consumers' contribution nor on the degree of common interest among the various participants. One views participation as essentially a management technique, whereas the other sees it as a means of affecting the distribution of power. It is clearly necessary to disentangle them.

The first claim basically asserts that getting consumers involved in decision-making will result in greater management efficiency. It is assumed that consumers will take part by providing new information to decision-makers about detailed or local problems with which they are particularly familiar. They can introduce both new intelligence about the likely effects of future decisions and feedback on past decisions, all of which is not easily attained by other means. As Klein and Lewis write, with respect to the health consumer:

He knows better about the quality of care even if he may know less about the quality of cure. He certainly is better able to tell whether health facilities are conveniently sited or whether the manners of health professionals are welcoming or coldly dictatorial. If the professionals's knowledge is less than total, so is the consumer's ignorance.[29]

Moreover, and of critical importance, it is additionally assumed that there is a general congruence of opinion between decision-makers and consumers concerning the desired policy results to be achieved. Both want to see provision of a good service: good housing, good schools, good health care and so forth. Consumer participation enables this common goal to be reached more efficiently, that is with least expenditure of effort or other resources. Since all interested parties want the same basic results, participation improves decisions from all points of view: the consumers gain greater satisfaction with their service, while the decision-makers gain the assurance that their decisions have been taken with the best relevant advice.

This essentially technical view is rarely opposed on the basis of its aims; few people are against efficiency *per se*. It is occasionally challenged however, on technical grounds. Decision-making is a complex and difficult activity and consumers' ability to improve decisions can be questioned. They not only lack appropriate training but also may be mistaken in their perceptions of local problems. With respect to planning, for instance,

> the questions which arise are quite often found to be economically and technically complex, and it is not always easy for the individual citizen to judge the real effects which plans are likely to have on his own circumstances.[30]

Some also claim that participation decreases management efficiency because it imposes considerable direct costs on the decision-making process. The addition of new people means that it takes longer to reach decisions, not only creating delays in instituting change but also entailing direct administrative costs in the time, and therefore salaries, of the officials involved. Where participation is introduced on a very controversial issue, resulting in considerable argumentation and debate, these costs can prove very substantial. Furthermore, creating a regular system for consumer input can be a considerable problem, as suggested by this discussion of social services departments:

> Even an annual exercise related to a regular review of the existing long-term plan is extremely time-consuming. To organise and to sustain a more prolonged and continuous effort to involve the public and local groups in the review and development of capital and revenue plans has had to be abandoned by more than one social services department.[31]

It may be noted that not everyone considers such delays to be a bad thing. The longer time taken to reach decisions may be viewed as a valuable brake on administrative machinery, giving everyone a chance to reflect seriously on the issues under question. In the case of health service administration 'delay may be seen as a beneficial device for saving the decision-makers from the consequences of their own mistakes by giving them time to correct course'.[32] Some would argue that considerable resources may indeed be saved by the introduction of participatory measures. By guiding policy away from misconceived ideas or false diagnoses of the problems under discussion, the new participants may save the costs which would be incurred in correcting decisions at a later date.

The second claim for participation goes well beyond the suggestion of increased efficiency in achieving common goals. It asserts that participation will change the very nature and direction of decisions by affecting the distribution of power between consumers and service providers. Consumers are assumed to play a much greater role than the mere provision of information; they will (and, in many eyes, should) use their involvement to direct more resources toward their own ends. It assumes, furthermore, that consumers' interests are not identical to those of the service providers; on the contrary, there is a clear conflict of interest between them. Consumers have strong views about the appropriate level and standards of their services, which are not matched by those providing them. Consumer participation, then, is an important device for shifting the balance of power in favour of the consumer.

Participation is commonly advocated expressly for this effect. It is argued that since it is the consumers who will bear the brunt of any decisions taken, policies should reflect their interests and not those of the service providers who do not have to live with them over time. Participation is a crucial means of protecting people from arbitrary decisions; it is 'the most effective defense against tyranny or counter to bureaucracy and centralisation. . . . It is only by participating that men can ensure that their interests are defended and promoted.'[33] This position is often phrased in terms of consumers' need for some form of protection from state monopolies. Given the fact that they cannot easily go elsewhere for their services, voting with their feet, such consumers are said to need some arrangement whereby they can express their preferences to the service providers 'as a form of customer audit'.[34] This was the principal basis for the advocacy of client participation in social services by the Seebohm Committee which argued, 'the consumer of the personal social services has limited choice among services and thus needs special opportunities to participate'.[35] Its report quoted the justification for consumer consultative machinery in nationalised industries, presented in a Consumer Council study, as having equal relevance for the personal social services:

> The purpose underlying the setting-up of the consultative machinery . . . is to meet the need of the consumers concerned for a means of bringing their influence to bear upon the industries . . . That there should exist this need of the consumers, however, derives in turn from the existence of limitations on their freedom of choice — the consumer's most compelling sanction against a supplier.[36]

One variant of this general position is the need to offer consumers some protection against the domination of decisions by entrenched professionals. This is stressed particularly in the health field; as R. G. S. Brown writes: 'There is a real risk that "consensus management" will be medically-dominated consensus and exclude patient and general public alike. . . . There is a need for local participation to prevent medical technology from having its own way.'[37]

It may be noted that this general argument for involving consumers in decisions in order to reflect their interests closely resembles the argument, presented above, concerning the *rights* of consumers to be involved. The difference is that here the focus is on the policy consequences of their participation, whereas in the earlier discussion it was on the importance of due process *per se*. The actual effects may, of course, be the same, and the two arguments are commonly conjoined.

But consumer participation is not only advocated on the grounds that it affects the distribution of power; it is also regularly opposed expressly for this reason. Three separate positions can be distinguished here. The first accepts the diagnosis that participation leads to greater consumer influence over decisions, but reverses the priority to be given to this group. Consumers represent only a minority of those affected by decisions, especially where they do not bear the relevant costs, and therefore their views should not be given undue weight. The elected or other decision-makers must balance consumers' needs with those of the wider community, it is argued, and it is they who should have full power to determine policy outcomes. Participation, in short, gives too much power to the participants. As Brown states, with respect to worker participation in the health field:

There is no obvious moral ground on which those sections of the public that happen to be employed in a public service should be given a larger opportunity to influence its development than the public at large, unless they possess distinctive and relevant professional skills.[38]

The second case against participation, based on its implications for the power of the respective participants, focusses on the practical limitations of finding representative spokesmen. Participation is a good idea in principle, it is suggested, but it cannot work effectively because representatives cannot be found who will speak for consumers as a whole. The participants will inevitably represent only minority interests, and their participation will therefore tend to damage general consumer satisfaction with their service rather than enhance it. Various reasons are offered for this dilemma. Some argue that the participants will be politically motivated; for instance, in the case of university students, 'the natural link of representation and responsibility is fractured, which means that such representatives will be tempted to engage in arbitrary decision-making and, more particularly, to indulge their ideological and personal prejudices.'[39] Others suggest that those who take part will inevitably be the articulate middle-class, and for this reason unrepresentative. Simmie, for instance, declares:

Those who participate in town planning, and consequently influence the distribution of those resources for which it is responsible, do not form a representative cross-section of society. . . . It is becoming generally accepted that nationally the poor, the sick, the old, the inadequate, the immobile and the under-housed characteristically do not compete in the struggle for power and resources.[40]

Finally, one variant of this position is that participants become unrepresentative through their participation. While their involvement should be encouraged, they may need to be watched: 'The informed tend to become the committed. We may need informed laymen to keep an eye on the specialist, and uninformed laymen to keep an eye on the informed.'[41]

In contrast, the third argument against participation on the grounds of its effects on the participants' respective power rests on a completely divergent assumption about the direction of its impact. It suggests that the interests of the new participants should be paramount, but that participation will work against them. Instead of increasing their overall ability to influence decisions, participation schemes will actually decrease their power, serving the interests of the service providers at the consumers' expense. Mechanisms for consumer participation are only 'talking shops', co-opting the participants and facilitating continued management control. This case is strongly stated by Colin Ward, in a discussion of tenant participation:

> Tenant 'consultation' and tenant 'participation' are so obviously designed as a means of manipulating tenants in the interests of housing management, that it is no wonder that nobody takes them seriously. They are the shadow, rather than the substance, of tenant control, and the tenants themselves, knowing that real power lies elsewhere, are not fooled. If anything, these token gestures, because they are not taken seriously, merely discredit the idea that people are capable of managing their own environment.[42]

This position also gains support from at least some Marxists. Cynthia Cockburn, for instance, writes: 'Whereas the firm tries to reduce market uncertainty by controlling demand, by intelligent advertising and judicious product design, the state uses participatory democracy and "the community approach". . . . Both are phases of corporate decision-making.'[43] It also underlies the message of the often-quoted French poster from 1968: 'Je participe, tu participes, ile participe, nous participons, vous participez, ils profitent.'[44]

Participation not only increases the immediate power of the service providers under this view; it also serves to protract their position by lending it a spurious legitimacy. Decision-makers can claim that consumers have been consulted, even where no weight is given to the concerns thereby expressed. This can prove a subtle and effective weapon against consumers' interests, even more so when minor concessions are made to them. As Saunders writes, such gains are 'highly charged symbolically, for they aid the legitimation of the political system itself by underlining the prevailing definition of it as pluralistic and accountable'.[45]

Finally, there is one further claim for consumer participation which is also concerned with the decisions stemming from it, but which has a very particular bias. This suggests that systems for participation, to the extent that they are decentralised, will generate greater diversity in service provision. It is argued that not all consumers want the same things, and that through a variety of decisions, arising from a variety of decision-making bodies including local consumers, some choice can be established. As one advocate of tenant participation states: 'there is . . . a case for ensuring that estates do not blend uniformly with one another, and indeed to try to break down existing large estates into recognisably different groups.'[46]

Consumer participation is also opposed on a converse argument. Diversity necessarily implies lack of identical treatment, and this may well prove inequitable, especially to those who are unable to press their case with any force. It is argued that decentralised participation arrangements necessarily favour the better-off and the articulate, resulting in even greater disadvantage for other consumers. As Batley writes, with respect to participation in planning:

> There is a danger that these areas [which do not demand a say in planning] could be jostled even further away from the resources and consideration as the more vocal areas which have always demanded attention take full advantage of their rights under the new system.[47]

The demand for participation

All of the major claims which have been made both for and against the introduction of participation have now been set out in terms of the specific issues which they raise. But there is yet another question which affects some views on this subject, namely the extent to which people really *want* to become involved in policy discussions. Is there, in other words, a demand for participation among the potential participants? This issue is crucial, since if they have no interest in taking part, there may be little point in establishing elaborate procedures to enable them to do so. A number of separate positions can be distinguished on this question.

First, many argue that people clearly have a great interest in becoming involved in the formulation of policies on issues of concern to them. In some views, this interest derives from a recognition of the developmental and expressive benefits from such involvement, whether the opportunity to gain new understanding of social issues or the simple immediate enjoyment of the discussions themselves. In others, it is seen to stem from a desire to contribute to the process of policy formation. In either case, there is no question of consumers' willingness to become involved; they are assumed to have an active desire to take part.

In direct contrast, others argue that few people have any interest in getting involved in the formulation of implementation of policy. From the participants' own point of view, participation imposes a considerable burden, taking them away from their families and other pleasures with no immediate gain for them. They have better things to do with their time. As Dahl writes: 'the cost is, plainly, that the time might be used in doing something else — often, in fact, something a great deal more interesting and important than going to a meeting'.[48] One variant of this general view is that people may take an initial interest in participation, if only for its novelty, but this will not be sustained over time. There is little reason to introduce elaborate measures for participation for the amount of consumer interest it will attract.

A middle route between these two positions suggests that people will wish to participate under certain circumstances. The desire to get involved is partly a reflection of particular personalities, not to mention family situations, but it will also vary with a person's sense of need to effect change and belief in his ability do so. Where people are satisfied with what is done for them, or alternatively believe that their efforts to get any changes will have no impact, they are unlikely to want to try to get involved. They must feel there are issues which need to be addressed, and forums where their contribution will be heard, in order to take the trouble to participate. They must also feel that they cannot more easily get the desired changes by other means, changing the 'supplier' of whatever it is they are dissatisfied with (their house or child's school or job). In other words, people will participate, and will want to participate, where the circumstances are right.[49]

A completely different position on this issue places little emphasis on what consumers actually want, but advocates participation on the grounds that it is good for them. People may be unaware of the benefits from participating, but these are none the less substantial. It is not anyway meaningful to respect their preferences before the event, for the act of participating will change these significantly. As Bachrach writes:

> [Participation] cannot be equated with sailing, money-making or theatre going; this means that it cannot be fitted into Bentham's

frame which supposedly enables one to choose rationally between alternative pleasures. . . . The unperceived effects of participation — upon individuals' outlook and personality, and upon their development into social beings — make the cost-benefit calculus for self-interest inappropriate.[50]

In other words, consumers will come to appreciate what participation has done for them, and be glad they were pushed into it, whatever their initial reaction to the idea.

Finally, others similarly disregard what consumers' wishes are in this matter, but argue that they should be required to participate for the common rather than their own particular, good. Whatever the benefits of participation for the individual participants, consumers' joint efforts are necessary to further general social welfare. As Braybrooke writes: 'Everyone stands to lose if the outcome is diminished by the failure of even one of the people eligible to participate to make his contribution, indeed the best contribution that he is capable of.'[51] Participation becomes, in sum, a social duty.

Summary and discussion

For those who seek a single and clear line of argument on a given issue, discussions of participation must prove the source of considerable frustration. The many positions presented in this chapter serve to illustrate why this should be so. Participation has been advocated and opposed on so many different bases that its proponents and critics only rarely meet on common soil. One is told that participation is good because it increases the capacities and self-confidence of the participants, but that it is bad because it serves to secure policies in the interests of the existing service providers. One is told that participation is bad because it gives too much power to unrepresentative minorities, but that it is good because it makes people think about others besides themselves. And so forth. There are, as has been shown, a jumble of arguments, from which it can prove difficult to extricate a head or a tail.

This chapter has tried to put these arguments into some semblance of logical order, representing one step in the direction of clarifying what participation is all about. It has not served to dispel all disagreement on this subject, however. Participation remains, at the end of it all, a matter of very considerable controversy, highly desirable to some and equally repugnant to others. But what should have begun to emerge from this extended discussion is some understanding of the sources of their disagreement, the reasons for conflicting stances on this question. There are, as has been shown, two very different bases to the debate.

First, it comes as no surprise that people approach the subject of participation, as any other, from different ideological positions. Not everyone shares the same goals or wants to further the interests of the same groups. A great deal of the controversy surrounding participation stems directly from this fact. With respect to the question of whose interests should be most heavily reflected in decisions, for instance, there is a clear split between advocates of the 'left' and those of the 'right'. The former tend to favour participation as a means of increasing consumer influence in the policy-making process. As consumers must bear the direct brunt of decisions taken, they argue, it is appropriate that their spokesmen play a major part in policy formulation. The latter, in contrast, tend to oppose participation on the grounds that consumer influence will be too great. It is the wider community who must bear the costs of decisions taken, they counter, and it is only fair that their spokesmen play the sole part in policy formulation. The two groups share a common analysis; the argument between them is simply about whose side they are on.

This ideological debate also manifests itself in discussions of other aspects of participation, not always leading, however, to identical conclusions. The positions of the 'left' and 'right' tend to reverse, for example, in considerations of the impact of participation on the social attitudes of those involved. Here, the former tend to oppose participation on the grounds that it co-opts the participants and makes them more accepting of established authority. The latter tend to favour it as a means of increasing the participants' sense of social responsibility and compliance with community norms. Again, the two groups share a common analysis; the argument between them again derives solely from whose side they are on.

But this is by no means the whole of the problem. Controversy over the desirability of participation does not stem solely from conflicting ideological perspectives. It arises also from differing diagnoses of the direction of its impact. There is, in fact, no consensus about what the consequences of participation actually are. While some assume, as indicated above, that participation serves to increase the influence of the participants over decisions, others argue that it has the opposite effect, decreasing their ability to make their views felt. Again, while some assume, as also indicated above, that participation increases the participants' sense of social responsibility, others assert that it reduces their willingness to comply with the existing social order. These arguments are not about conflicting values; they are not resolved by sorting out whose interests are to be taken into account. They arise from conflicting analyses, from differing expectations about what happens when participation is introduced. They are of quite a different order.

There is no need to explain the fact that people with different values approach participation in different ways. It is to be expected that some will favour its introduction and some oppose it. There is also no need to explain the differential stress given to its varying effects, some focussing on its developmental consequences and others on its ramifications for policy. It is again to be expected that people place different weights on the achievement of different goals. What does require explanation, however, is the lack of agreement on what participation actually brings about. It is logically impossible for all the claims reviewed above to be correct. Participation cannot act both to serve consumers' material interests *and* to damage them; it cannot make the participants both more conservative *and* more radical. If the impact of participation is to be understood, these conflicting claims must somehow be reconciled. It is to this end that the following chapter is devoted.

5   Analysing participation

What is participation all about? What does it achieve? The claims have been reviewed, but no simple answer has emerged with any clarity. On the contrary, a variety of conflicting assertions have been found to co-exist uneasily in discussions of this question. Proffered frequently with great confidence, they appear to have a stamp of certainty about them. But such claims are not established fact; indeed, given the incompatibility of their conclusions, they could not all be true. Whatever the conviction with which they are asserted, they should be seen only as hypotheses about the results stemming from participation.

This chapter elaborates a different sort of hypothesis about the impact of participation. Through an analysis of the processes set in motion by its introduction, it argues that the consequences of participation are highly unpredictable. One cannot assume particular results on the basis of either the intentions of the participants or the specific structures through which they are involved. Furthermore, because of the complex nature of the interests mobilised by participation, one cannot even say whose interests are best served. This unpredictability, however, helps to explain the analytical dilemma posed by the existence of conflicting claims; they cannot all be right after the event, but they all make sense before it. The logic of this argument must now be set out in some detail.

The centrality of bargaining

What does participation really entail? In Chapter 2, consumer participation was defined as the introduction of a new set of people, the consumers, into the process of formulating or implementing decisions —

in the context of interest here, decisions on social policy. Bringing new people into policy deliberations means the introduction of a whole new set of aims and considerations, adding to those already around the table. People do not enter into the process, any more than any other, with a blank slate. They have their own particular interests, their own hopes and worries, their own ways of looking at the problems at hand. They may get involved in order to work for clearly specified goals; even where they do not, they are likely to develop some with the passage of time. This is the case not only for the new participants, the consumers, but also for the pre-existing ones, the service providers. Both groups, in sum, have some interests which they will seek to further through the activity of participation. And, although it is logically possible for their goals to be strictly congruent with one another, they will rarely be so. Some controversy, some conflicts over the direction policies should take, can reasonably be expected. Participation, then, entails the introduction of new — and to some extent conflicting — interests into the decision-making process.

But participation is not only about the mobilisation of new interests; it is also about how people go about trying to realise them. There are, in practice, two distinct types of consumer participation: direct participation, where the consumers have some direct contact with those responsible for making or implementing decisions, and indirect participation, where they do not. This distinction, elaborated in Chapter 2, is not an arbitrary one; although the motivation for participating may be similar in the two instances, there are crucial differences between them in the processes involved.

Where participation is indirect, both the consumer participants and the other decision-makers may try to pursue their respective goals, but they do not — indeed they cannot — do so together. To the extent that the aims of each entail some concessions from the other, they may each try their best to win these, but they are unable to negotiate, either individually or as a group, in order to do so. In the absence of direct personal contact, both groups are, by definition, isolated from one another. They have no means of discussing either what they want or what sorts of compromise might prove acceptable. The consumers may vote, campaign or write letters to their newspaper to indicate their preferences; the service providers may undertake campaigns, put out publicity or issue advice to indicate theirs. Indeed, the latter may sponsor surveys or set up referenda to solicit information on consumer opinion. But neither group has direct access to the other, and this places considerable limits on their opportunities to engage in success-ful strategic action.

Where participation is direct, in contrast, the consumers and service providers are, by definition, actively involved with one another and can pursue their respective interests together. The existence of some contact enables them to negotiate, either individually or as a group, in order to achieve their desired ends. They can discuss what they want and what concessions they are willing to make; they can try to put their views forward in the most convincing light; they can respond, and respond quickly, to the gambits of the other side. Direct participation, in short, facilitates *bargaining* between the consumers and decision-makers, and this opportunity to deploy strategic action changes the nature of the participatory process dramatically. The introduction of direct participation can indeed be seen as the introduction of an arena in which such activities can take place. It is this form of participation — and indeed this bargaining process — with which this analysis is primarily concerned.

As the concept of bargaining is so central to this discussion, it is important to clarify exactly what it means. First, a formal definition is in order. Bargaining represents a subset, although quite a large one, of the many activities encompassed by strategic behaviour. The essence of the latter is the existence of interdependence between the persons involved so that the decisions of each are contingent on estimates of the decisions of the other. Bargaining involves attempts to reach par-ticular conclusions under these conditions; it has been defined as:

> a means by which two or more purposive actors arrive at specific outcomes in situations in which: (1) the choices of the actors will determine the allocation of some value(s), (2) the outcome for each participant is a function of the behaviour of the other(s), and (3) the outcome is achieved through negotiations between or among the players.[1]

But what does the term 'bargaining' really mean in practice? In fact, it describes all sorts of actions on the part of the respective par-ticipants, not all of which — indeed perhaps few of which — would be viewed by them in this light. It does not simply mean haggling; it includes any attempts by the parties involved to influence the thinking and activities of others. While not excluding direct bargaining, the term is used fairly loosely to refer to any behaviour directed at gaining some concessions from the other side. Of course, instances of explicit bargaining can be found, such as where consumers agree to stop pressing for one set of demands on the basis that others will be met. But a much wider range of behaviour is also encompassed by this term. Simply being friendly may go a long way to getting certain results in some circumstances; being unfriendly or 'difficult' may equally achieve the same results in others. Indeed, some activities may not obviously be relevant to the topic at hand. Thus, the carefully timed joke, the repetitive speech, even the delayed arrival can all be interpreted as examples of strategic, or bargaining, behaviour. In practice, it may be difficult to distinguish intended consequences from unintended ones: a long speech may be intended as a filibuster or it may be the result of inexperience or fatigue; a trip to the lavatory may be timed to avoid a particular agenda item or it may simply correspond to a call of nature. But these are practical problems of inference which do not detract from the general characterisation of the process as a bargaining one. It must be added, in passing, that no pejorative overtones are intended by the use of this term; it is meant to be purely descriptive of a process by which people try collectively to achieve their aims.

Furthermore, it should be stressed that the use of the term 'bargaining' in this context should not be taken to imply that the only questions at issue are the attainment of goods or services. The interests of the consumers or the decision-makers are not — or need not be — material only; they include a range of concerns from the more long-term goals of those they represent to their own immediate welfare. Consumers are likely, of course, to want to effect certain policies regarding their services, but they are likely also to have other aspirations. They may seek information on future plans, wish to create good will, hope to foster more understanding attitudes or aim to develop their own skills and capacities, to name just a few. Equally, the service providers are likely to want to effect certain policies, preferably with consumer approval, but they, too, will have other goals. They, too, may seek to influence consumers' ideas and interests, also aim to generate good will, hope to engender 'responsible' attitudes and, where they are elected, solicit votes. A wide range of interests are at stake in any bargaining process. It is a central characteristic of that process that they can all be sought at the same time.

Some may feel that the concept of bargaining implies too much calculation on the part of the participants — and too little willingness to work together on issues of common concern. Surely, they may say, participation entails greater co-operation and good will among the participants than implied by this term. And, indeed, some writers do characterise participation exactly in this way. Roberts and his colleagues, for instance, explicitly distinguish the processes involved in worker participation from those of collective bargaining, both in the relationship or attitudes of the two sides and in what goes on between them. Collective bargaining entails a clear 'adversarial' relationship: 'Each side knows that, though they may be compelled by circumstances and law to recognise that mutual advantage lies in agreeing with each other, a gain for one may be a loss to the other. . . .' The process of participation, in contrast, 'is based on the principle that managers and employees share to a large extent a common interest and that there is mutual advantage in its recognition'. The means by which decisions are reached is also assumed to differ in the two circumstances; in collective bargaining, there are demands and responses so that 'the process of arriving at the final decision is then one of bargained exchanges about previously made decisions until accommodation is reached, and a period of peace is bought.' In the case of participation, in contrast, 'participation is more continuous through time . . . [as decisions are made] by an input of information and analysis over a lengthy period. . . . It is a cumulative process.'[2]

Other writers similarly define their terms more strictly, indicating other ways of reaching conclusions than a simple bargain. Brian Barry, for instance, contrasts 'bargaining' and 'discussion on merits'. Whereas the former involves threats of inducements, the latter is more amicable: 'the parties to the dispute set out . . . to reach an agreement on what is the morally right division, what policy is in the interests of all of them or will promote the most want-satisfaction, and so on.'[3] J. R. Lucas also makes a distinction between a 'bargain' and a 'compromise' in terms of the state of mind of the participants. Whereas the former is reached purely by concessions, with no effort to see things from the other's point of view, the latter is more complex:

> In a compromise the parties agree on a course of action which neither of them thinks entirely desirable but each prefers to the one the other wants. . . . In reaching a compromise, each party needs to explain what his order of priorities is, and to be prepared to give way on some points in order to win concessions on others. But it is not a simple bargain. It is an endeavour to see things from the other's point of view, to internalize his system of values, and to

find a course of action which should rate fairly high whether evaluated by him or by oneself.[4]

These distinctions usefully highlight the various ways in which two groups may approach each other in the course of joint discussions, but all are readily encompassed by any participation exercise. What is really at issue here is a question of attitudes, both before deliberations have begun and after they have taken place. Do the various parties come together as colleagues or as adversaries? Do they feel that the decisions they reach are morally right or simply the best they could get in the circumstances? The assumption of this analysis, elaborated more fully below, is that they do and feel both — that the two sides are on some occasions highly divided and on others happy partners. It depends on the issues, their previous discussions and the ways in which those involved undertake their task. Furthermore, working together may be a genuine concern or it may be a subtle bargaining ploy; attempts to convince a fellow participant that a decision is the 'right' one can be viewed, for instance, in either light. The term 'bargaining' has been used here to indicate the presence of some conflict, but it should not be taken to imply that relations are altogether hostile. On the contrary, discussions may frequently take place in a very friendly atmosphere.

Participation has been described as the introduction of a new set of participants into the process of decision-making. The activities in which they engage — the bargaining, discussion on merits, cumulative information-building and so forth — take place whether or not the new participants take part in them. They are in the processes which are set in motion whenever decisions need to be taken and there are differences of opinion among those involved. The introduction of new participants simply complicates the picture. The dramatic nature of these processes has been vividly described by one writer on decision-making:

> At the outset begins the process of discussion, perhaps aimed at understanding, but invariably aimed at crystallizing opinion on the next action. We presume that it becomes more intense, probably more devious, more heated, and in any case more protracted, as group attention to the unresolved problem continues. Of course, the higher the perceived stakes given the values of the participants, the greater the fervour in haggling. . . . Finally the prospect of making concessions is always available. . . .[5]

So it is in the case of participation.

Bargaining outcomes and the problem of power

When people sit down to bargain, they do not know how it will turn out. The result, in formal language, is indeterminate. The respective parties may find that they can easily reach a happy compromise; they may find, alternatively, that one party's position is in fact wholly desirable; or they may find that no common ground exists between them at all. Decisions may be made or they may be delayed; the respective parties may be content with the outcome or they may be disappointed. Both, of course, hope to win their case in advance of their discussions, but neither can be certain of doing so. Participation does not ensure any given result.

But what about the importance of power? It is often argued that, whatever the rhetoric attached to participation exercises, the respective parties have unequal power and consequently the outcome of their deliberations is not, in fact, so open. The consumer participants, it is asserted, have little or no leverage compared with the other decision-makers. They are the invited guests at a party stage-managed by their official hosts, and can only pass comment on details pertaining to their situation. Their involvement, it is said, can make little impact for these reasons. Indeed, as discussed at the end of Chapter 2, a number of writers have attempted to incorporate the concept of power into their definitions of participation in order to demonstrate its centrality.

Certainly it is true that the new participants and the experienced decision-makers do not meet on equal terms. While participation should not be defined according to the participants' power, it is crucial to recognise the nature of their respective positions. It is likely, indeed, that the consumer participants will have an uphill struggle to gain their own ends, derived from a combination of their inexperience and their lack of a clearly established position in the decision-making process. But the decision-makers do not hold all the cards, and it cannot be assumed that they will inevitably get their way. Both the processes of negotiation and the nature of the interests brought to that process are considerably more complicated. These issues must be analysed with some care.

The imbalance in the positions of the official decision-makers and the new participants is easily demonstrated. The former have considerable experience of committees and other meetings, of handling agendas and official reports, and using a range of well-known tactics to gain their way. It would be surprising if they were not more adept at deploying strategic behaviour than any newcomers, given their experience of doing so in the course of their ordinary political and administrative activities. Furthermore, the new participants are likely to be conscious of their own lack of familiarity with many issues and problems, and to defer — at least for a time — to those who appear to have expertise. They cannot become equal partners, or even equal adversaries, overnight.

But power is not a characteristic which can be carefully measured in advance of any confrontation. It is composed of all the resources which any group can muster to win its case, and the consumer participants have a range of such resources on which they can call. They can threaten to engage in activities which would be thought damaging by the other decision-makers, such as staging demonstrations during sensitive election periods. Conversely, they can offer the inducement of support on difficult issues, using the organised help of their own associations. Possibly more effectively, they can attempt to widen the number of interests aroused by particular issues, publicising — and therefore politicising — the official stance, and bringing new groups into the debate. On a more subtle level, the consumers may prove able to argue their case in terms of the interests of the service providers, winning the latter around to their own perspective. A clever spokesman can wield a great deal of power by sheer argument, combined with careful observation of the aims and assumptions of the other side.

Furthermore, the ability of both groups to deploy these resources is likely to grow over time. As consumers and decision-makers gain familiarity with each other's concerns through their interaction, each will become more able to present their own case in the most convincing light. While they are not typically strangers in this respect when they begin, they are certainly not so after the passage of time. This has been clearly described in the context of officer—member discussions in local government:

> Each side can therefore make calculations which strike a balance between what they want and what they know each is willing and able to accept. The technocrat is not offering disembodied advice but framing his recommendations in the knowledge of prevailing conditions, and prominent among these conditions are the preferences and predilections of the committee chairman, the committee itself, and the majority of the council.[6]

Similar processes also pertain in consumer—member and consumer—officer relationships in the context of participation schemes. As the consumers start with a possible disadvantage, because of their relative inexperience with the committee process, this time factor may be particularly beneficial to them. As one experienced parent governor has observed about parental involvement:

> If you bring on to governing bodies the kind of people who are interested in what goes on in the school, they'll be just that. . . .
> How fast people learn all the subtle ways in which the system tries to discipline them. How remarkably they learn to resist such discipline, even when it is reinforced by all the power that comes from access to information and control of information.[7]

But to designate the participatory process as a simple power struggle between two opposing sides is to misunderstand the essential nature of the interests involved. While the aims of the consumers and other decision-makers are unlikely to be strictly congruent, they are also rarely strictly conflicting. If they held no interests in common, it would be reasonable to depict them locked in battle, each aiming to win as much ground as possible from the opposing side. Indeed, if their interests coincided exactly, there would be no battle, but only a common meeting-point to agree future plans. But in most situations, there are some interests which they hold in common and some which they hold alone. There is, in short, a partial battle and a partial meeting ground; the extent to which one or the other exists will change according to the issue.

There are many examples which could be given to demonstrate these overlapping interests. Officials frequently aim to increase the scope of activities covered by their particular department, if not their budgets, and this coincides with the general interest among consumers to gain additional services. Indeed, elected members often come to identify with particular services, such as housing or personal social services, and seek to extend their scope in the same way as officers. Both groups may also be consumers of the relevant services, and therefore sympathise with the consumer position from their own personal experience. On the other hand, both officials and elected members have some aims which are in direct conflict with those of consumers. Whereas the latter want to keep down any charges which they have to pay, the former are likely to be more concerned about the general increase in rates or taxes which this would entail. Again, both groups responsible for administering a service will have some ideas about what policies should be, which may conflict with the views of consumers, either regularly or from time to time. Similarly, there may be divergent opinions about particular aspects of any agreed policy, such as the location of an amenity or the specific nature of facilities to be provided.

In addition to these general sources of both compatibility and conflict *between* groups, however, it is also common for there to be sources of conflict *within* individual groups. It cannot be assumed that either all consumers or all decision-makers hold a single agreed position on every issue. Consumers may come into conflict over the distribution of resources between different client groups or between geographic locations within one given area. Officers of different departments may bring divergent perspectives to their discussions and therefore pursue conflicting aims. Elected members may clash both on party lines and in the course of furthering the interests of their respective constituents. Members of all groups may also simply have differing views about what policies ought to be, based on differing personal values or experiences. There are, in sum, many additional sources of cleavage besides the obvious one of the broad groups which the participants represent.

Consumers and decision-makers, then, generally have some conflicting and some congruent interests which will be reflected in their joint discussions about policy. They confront each other neither as simple adversaries nor as friendly colleagues but as some combination of the two. This has been colourfully described in a discussion of consumer participation in health provision:

> Both producers and consumers are a very mixed bag; and there are competing and conflicting interests within each group. Instead of looking at their relationship in terms of a Cowboys and Indians conflict, it is therefore much more accurate to picture it as an elaborately choreographed ballet — with the dancers constantly changing partners and adopting new formations as the setting of the drama changes.[8]

Such changing alliances do not develop solely because of attention to different issues; they arise also because attitudes and interests can change in the course of debate. As Bachrach writes, focussing on the new participant: 'Changes in interest might occur not only because of the force of the argument presented at the forum but also because of a personal involvement in the participatory process which may significantly change one's attitude, perspective, and value priorities.'[9] Such arguments hold equally for the other groups involved in the participatory process.

Furthermore, the committee process itself tends to diminish the strength of individual affiliations. This arises partly because the existence of overlapping interests provides a potential for co-operation on which each group is likely to call. It is helped by the freedom which committee members, both consumers and service providers, typically have to act as they see fit. Although they may need to justify their position to others at some later point, their hands are rarely tied by either written or spoken promises to a wider audience. But finally, the inherent character of small group discussions discourages tenacity to a single view. As Dahl writes:

> Indeed, committee democracy is, typically, hostile to partisanship. For the committee reflects the familiar psychological needs of small and intimate groups. Committee members may begin as strangers but they are soon acquaintances and, in time, friends. . . . Committee democracy is typically, then, consensual democracy. The members strive for unanimity, particularly on important questions. They do not try to crush an opponent, they try instead to win him over.[10]

The effect of such discussions can be described in terms of sheer power, but the processes by which such effects are reached are much more subtle.

The act of wielding of power, then, is a very complex business, and its effects difficult to predict. But, as explored in Chapter 2, 'power' should not be confused with 'powers'. The latter refers to the formal responsibilities delegated to any individual or decision-making body, the issues over which decisions may be taken without recourse to ratification or amendment by others. Consumer participation schemes vary in the degree to which they provide consumers any formal powers. The bodies in which consumers are involved may have many or few decision-making powers and the consumers themselves may have a full or only partial status with respect to them. Generally, however, consumers' powers are fairly limited. Perhaps, it might be argued, it is this fact which makes some writers describe participation schemes as ineffective from the consumers' point of view.

It is certainly true that the presence or absence of some formal powers helps those who have the privilege of holding them. Where consumers participate in bodies with few decision-making powers, or where their status does not entail voting rights, they have, by definition, few formal powers. It is therefore easy to argue that they have little power, that they are basically at the mercy of those with formal powers, whether involved with them or elsewhere. This may be so, but it cannot be assumed from the start. As long as they are able to convince those with such powers of the merits of their case, or to worry them sufficiently about the consequences of taking other action that the desired decisions are taken, they can be seen to have effective power — whatever their formal status. Conversely, where consumers participate in bodies with many decision-making powers and have full voting status in them, they have, by definition, some formal powers. It might be argued that they therefore have some power, that they can affect the course of decisions taken. Again, this may prove to be the case, but again it cannot be assumed from the start. As long as the other decision-makers are able to convince them of the merits of their case, or to worry them sufficiently about the consequences of taking other action that their desired decisions are taken, the consumer can be seen to have little effective power — despite their formal status.

What is being argued here is that no exact correspondence between consumers' formal powers and their effective power can be assumed. All systems for consumer participation may enable consumers to wield some power, to get in practice what they want, and all may enable power to be exercised against them. Neither they nor the service providers can be certain of the direction such power will take. The only statement that can be made with certainty is that systems for consumer participation provide an arena in which consumers and service providers can vie with one another to achieve their desired ends. Through the careful exercise of strategic action, either group may prove more successful in obtaining their aims.

This problem has been formally explored by game theorists with similar conclusions. Game theory is the study of strategic choice and its consequences in circumstances whose outcomes are not based primarily on either skill or chance. In its own terms, it is concerned with 'games of strategy' which are those 'in which the best course of action for each player depends on what the other players do'.[11] The decisions of the respective parties are thereby interdependent, that is, they are based on each party's respective expectations of the others' actions.

Game theory has traditionally been applied in the context of an assumption of pure conflict of interests between the relevant parties. This situation is described as a zero-sum game because any gain made by one party is necessarily off-set by a corresponding loss by the other, the total summing to zero. More recently, however, game theory has been extended to a consideration of other situations; it has been pointed out that while the zero-sum game is the limiting case of pure conflict, the 'pure collaboration' game is the limiting case of exact congruence of interests. In this case 'the players win or lose together, having identical preferences regarding the outcome.'[12] In contrast to these two extreme cases, there is the non-zero-sum game, where the respective parties have some conflicting interests and some congruent ones. In these circumstances, any losses sustained by one party may not be identical to any gains by the other, and indeed the outcome may include gains by both parties, although not necessarily of equivalent size; in other words, the total does not equal zero. Winning in this situation implies 'gaining relative to one's own value system' which may be accomplished 'by bargaining, by mutual accommodation, and by the avoidance of mutually damaging behaviour'.[13]

Game theorists have found that the results of non-zero-sum games are not predictable, for there are a range of solutions which involve both sides gaining according to their own value systems. As Sen writes: 'Both gain from cooperation, but one gains more with some contracts than others, while the other gains less with those. That is what the bargain is about.'[14] There is no single equilibrium point at which each side cannot improve its position. The eventual outcome is dependent on the choice of strategies employed by the respective parties, and game theorists have been unable to develop general theories for predicting strategic choice in this circumstance.

It has been demonstrated above that the interaction of consumers and decision-makers in participatory discussions is equivalent to a non-zero-sum game. The two groups have some conflicting interests and some congruent ones; both thereby serve to gain from negotiations, although they will not necessarily gain equally. Arrangements for consumer participation enable the respective groups to discuss together any number of issues of common concern to them, in other words, to bargain. The result may be a happy agreement, a less happy compromise, or total stalemate. No single outcome can be assumed from the start.

The 'open' nature of the participatory situation has been emphasised here, in part as an antidote to those who insist that it is wholly 'closed'. But having made the point, it is necessary to back-track slightly. Formal powers are not the same as effective power, but they are not entirely without meaning. Consumers and decision-makers do not typically confront one another with identical powers, and the imbalance in favour of the latter must give them an advantage. Many participation exercises grant consumers only an advisory or consultative status, so that their views can be ignored when issues are put to a vote. More seriously, many such exercises do not take place in the forum where decisions are eventually taken, so that whatever the consumers' influence on those they participate with, their views may not be force-fully transmitted to those who count. For these reasons alone, consumers may well prove to have unequal power, to be less able to attain their full aims compared with those with greater formal powers. But through their involvement in direct discussions, they have considerable oppor-tunity to win decision-makers around to their point of view. They may not be wholly powerful, but they are by no means wholly powerless.

At the outset of this chapter, attention was drawn to the distinction between systems for direct and indirect participation, based on the existence of any direct contact between consumers and decision-makers. It was suggested, and it must be reiterated, that the crucial difference between them lies in the greater opportunities for effective bargaining afforded by direct schemes. This analysis, in other words, applies primarily to systems for direct participation — council com-mittees, management boards, advisory committees and so forth. It is the direct contact, in a necessarily limited forum, between consumers and decision-makers which enables them to undertake effective strategic action.

Where participation is limited to indirect means, whether initiated by consumers or decision-makers, the opportunities for either side to engage in strategic behaviour are much more limited. The isolation from one another means, by definition, that no discussions can take place in which efforts to persuade, induce, cajole or otherwise influence the other might be undertaken. Of course, they may try to do any or all of these things by indirect means — letters to the press, public cam-paigns, leafleting and so forth — but there is no forum in which com-promises and concessions can be ironed out. Furthermore, unless such participatory activities are undertaken collectively, by groups of parents or local residents' associations and so forth, they are unlikely to prove very effective. Individual indirect efforts are all too easily ignored.

Not all arrangements for direct participation will function in the same way, however, and some distinguishing factors may be noted. The sheer number of participants, from either side, is likely to prove significant, affecting credibility and representativeness if too small and the ability to hold effective discussions if too large. Continuity of membership is also likely to be important, influencing in subtle ways the relationships around a discussion table. The physical layout of the meeting room can affect the semblance of equality and the ease with which any degree of intimacy can be achieved. Finally, and much more importantly, the extent to which the participation forum is itself empowered to make decisions is likely to affect the zeal of — and consequently the efforts made by — the participants. For all of these reasons, on-going committees will prove much more effective arenas for bargaining than occasional public meetings, although both are forms of direct participation.

Finally, this analysis of the complexities of the distribution of power has not even begun to tackle the equally formidable problem of its identification. Having established that participation schemes entail the exercise of power, the next step may be thought to be a discussion of how it might be traced. This is an exceedingly difficult task, even for those directly involved, for its usage can prove highly subtle. As Partridge writes:

> It is not easy to make the necessary discriminations; it is so difficult in fact that very often the participants themselves, the man who exercises power and the man over whom it is exercised, do not themselves know whether sanctions are being employed, and whether there is an element of . . . 'domination' in their relationship.[15]

How much more complicated is the multi-person situation, with potentially changing alliances and interests, than the two-person one.

The problem of identifying the exercise of power was discussed in Chapter 2, but it may be useful to review it briefly here. It was shown that at least three different positions have been put forward on this issue. Power may be attributed to those who gain particular decisions which they wanted, to those who manage to restrict or stifle discussion of issues which they did not want considered, or to those who alter the perceived interests of others to coincide with their own. All of these manifestations of power can be found, of course, in the context of systems for consumer participation. Decisions may be taken which are in the interests of one particular group. Decisions, or even discussions about them, may also be avoided by the successful manipulation of agendas. Finally, the perceived interests of the respective participants may be altered in the course of their deliberations.

In practice, all of these outcomes are more easy to state than to prove. There may be blatant cases, even quite a few of them, where the service providers or consumers clearly get their own way. Plans get made, votes get taken, and the resulting policies visibly benefit one group or another. But there are also many occasions where the 'winner' is not so clear-cut, especially where the interests of the various groups shade into one another. Indeed, in many formal committees, decisions are not even put to a vote. This has been termed 'decision by interpretation', occurring where 'one of the actors simply interprets what he or she considers to be the essence of the discussion and this interpretation is then tacitly accepted by the other actors'.[16] Where this happens, it is particularly difficult to identify the exercise of power, that is who got his way, for the participants themselves may not have clearly formulated their own final positions.

The analysis of the processes entailed by the introduction of participation is now complete. Implementing participation means bringing in new people, with their own aspirations, problems and ways of looking at the world, to the decision-making process. The aims of these new people, the consumers in this analysis, are not identical to those of the people already engaging in it, but they are also not wholly conflicting. In the course of discussing policies, the two groups, the new and the old, will bargain with one another in attempts to secure as many different goals as they can. The outcome will reflect their respective power, but it is likely to prove exceedingly difficult to demonstrate who was more successful in attaining their ends.

The claims for participation reviewed

Given this interpretation of the participatory process, what light can be shed on the claims for participation set out in the preceding chapter? It is now possible to review the assertions commonly made about the impact of participation, and consider their cogency. It was emphasised that some of these were logically incompatible, and no amount of analysis can magically reconcile these. But the conclusions drawn here can help to explain how such conflicting expectations ever came to be held. They may not all be correct, but at least they can each make sense in their own terms.

The first case for (and against) the introduction of consumer participation differed from the others by making no claim about the results it would achieve. It was argued that consumers have a basic right to participate in decisions which affect them or, conversely, that those who bear the costs of these decisions (i.e. the taxpayers) should have the sole right to determine their outcome. This analysis cannot help to settle these claims, for they do not rest on assertions about the outcome of participatory discussions. Although proponents of each view might believe that better decisions would result from the process in their respective case, this is not the grounds on which their case is made. It rests solely on the assertion of basic rights and the importance of due process.

All other claims, however, rested on expectations about the results which participation would achieve, and this analysis can be seen to have some relevance to them. First, a range of arguments focussed on the developmental effects for the new participants. Participation was seen to bring consumers both greater personal fulfilment and more developed capacities, and to provide the source of immediate 'expressive' benefits. Most viewed these as positive effects, but some feared that they would lull consumers into too great an acceptance of their situation.

Whatever the value attached to these results, is it reasonable to expect them to follow from participation? It is easily argued that participation, particularly in the limited sphere under consideration here, is not the only route to these developmental ends, and furthermore that its contribution in this respect cannot be assured. As one analyst has asserted, using the more formal terminology of logical exposition, participation is neither necessary nor sufficient for the development of people's moral capacities:

> It is not necessary, for it is perfectly possible that a man have a vision of the common good and yet not take part in government or politics. Indeed, this often occurs when men believe that government is in tolerably good hands and that the common good will not be better served by their participation. Nor is it sufficient, for many who participate are not conspicuously better developed morally than those of us who do not. Nor is participation necessary for

development of one's sense of self-esteem, for many persons who do not participate are not racked by doubts about their worth and doubtless many who do participate are prey to such doubts.[17]

Yet to state such a case is not to suggest that participation cannot or does not ever make a contribution to individual development, whether moral, emotional or intellectual. It is, in fact, quite reasonable to expect that the processes of participation will lead to such ends, both when it is indirect and, possibly more forcefully, when it is direct. In the latter case, it has been shown that participation tends to entail both considerable discussion of issues, including the explicit or implicit weighing of various priorities, and the potential exercise of some strategic actions. It seems likely that in the course of such deliberations the participants will learn a good deal about their own and others' modes of thinking about issues, their relative priorities and the constraints under which policies must be decided. In addition, it is likely that they will gain an increased ability to navigate the difficult waters of the committee process, to manage their own and their fellow members' reactions to particular problems. They may well develop, in sum, a much wider knowledge of the issues with which they must deal and an increased capacity to deal with them. Such changes may also bring in their wake an increased self-confidence, and this may indeed, as asserted by some, spill over to a much broader range of issues. It may also, of course, prove to be the source of both immediate pleasure and more long-term fulfilment.

Nor is the process of development solely one way. The presence of some consumer participants is unlikely to go unnoticed by the other decision-makers with whom they are involved. They will tend to watch the reactions of the newcomers, learn how they think and what sorts of aims they hold. This may lead them to reconsider their own assumptions and to develop their capacities for responding to new situations. They, too, may gain both immediate pleasure and more long-term fulfilment from the introduction of participation. While rarely stated as an explicit reason for implementing participation, certain developmental effects for the decision-makers may well occur.

In the case of indirect participation, in contrast, such results — on both sides — are less easily obtained. In the absence of direct interaction with the service-providers, the individual consumer does not have the same sources of information and ideas about issues as the direct participant. Furthermore, he has more limited opportunities for developing his capacities to manage a decision-making environment, to sharpen his skills at debate and discussion. But this is not to suggest that *no* learning or development can take place in the absence of direct interaction. To the extent that consumers familiarise themselves with issues or candidates in order to campaign or vote in elections, for instance, some learning will take place. Through discussions with each other, they may well increase their own debating abilities, and possibly more comfortably in the presence solely of their peers. They may also gain both long-term fulfilment and immediate enjoyment from the activities in which they engage. None the less, they lack exposure to a particular source of stimulation — the existing decision-makers — compared with the direct participant. The same considerations hold, of course, in the case of indirect initiatives by the service providers.

A second set of claims concerning participation, related to its developmental effects for the participants, focussed on the changes their involvement would bring about in their subsequent attitudes and behaviour. Two contrasting views were offered here. Some suggested that participation would serve to increase the legitimacy consumers ascribe to their political institutions, making them more willing to comply with policies imposed by those in positions of authority. In a similar vein, some argued that participation would increase consumers' sense of responsibility for their environment, decreasing their propensity to engage in anti-social behaviour. In contrast, others argued that participation would have a converse effect, making consumers less compliant instead of more, and more willing to confront the existing system. The extent to which such effects were welcomed or opposed varied, of course, with the political stance of the individual analyst.

How do such opposing views come to be held about the same phenomenon? And which analysis is correct? The differing expectations arise from differing assumptions about both the attitudes of the participants *ex ante* and the nature of the process in which they are engaged. The first view, that participation leads to greater social integration, rests on the twin assumptions that the participant consumers have little sense of integration prior to their involvement and that the service providers are all concerned to foster this sense. Additionally, it assumes that the concerns of the latter — to integrate or control the consumer population — will automatically prevail. The second view, that participation leads to reduced social integration, rests on the converse assumption that the participant consumers are generally politically passive prior to their involvement, but will be fired into activism by their exposure to new issues and people. It is not conversely assumed that the service providers wish to foster such a change, but solely that their effectiveness will be limited.

Both sets of expectations, despite – or properly because of – their varying assumptions, may prove correct in some cases. The prior attitudes and behaviour of the consumer participants are unlikely to be solely of one kind. Indeed, and this is not typically assumed by writers on this issue, the same holds for the service providers as well. While some consumers will approach participation with a concern to confront the existing social order, others will be equally strong defenders of it. Some will see participation as a means of generating greater activism among their peers; others will be equally concerned to make them more 'responsible'. The latter may be particularly evident where the anti-social behaviour of others affects them directly, such as rowdy children in their children's schools or tenant vandalism on their estates. Similarly, while the service providers are unlikely to want to lose their particular positions, some will be concerned to foster a more questioning attitude on the part of consumers. Indeed, the more radical elected members may view participation as a useful training ground for consumers to learn how to 'take on' the system from the inside. The concerns of both sides, in other words, are not monolithic; there is a range of interests which will be mobilised by any participation exercise.

But whatever the concerns of the respective parties, these analyses are misled by their assumption that particular viewpoints will prevail. It should not be assumed that either the consumers or the service providers will automatically get their way. The process of participation entails no mechanism by which the aims of either can be assured. Through discussions of the constraints under which decisions must be taken, formerly vociferous consumers may be tamed into acceptance of the existing system. But equally, through exposure to the processes by which decisions normally get taken, formerly passive consumers may be fired into greater activism and become less compliant with existing norms. The same holds in the case of the service providers; they, too, may be radicalised by their exposure to consumers' viewpoints or they may turn more conservative. Participation, as discussed at length above, entails the interaction of the two groups and provides the opportunity for them to bargain with one another. The outcome of this process on the attitudes of the participants is simply not predictable from the outset; many expectations are reasonable, but no one is certain.

Finally, the last, and possibly most important, set of claims for participation focussed not on its effects on the individuals involved but on its impact on policy. As in the preceding case, a number of divergent diagnoses were found to be housed together under this general focus on policy decisions, again sharing neither common assumptions nor common expectations. Some argued that consumer participation in decision-making would lead to better decisions through the contribution of new ideas and information from the consumer side. All groups were assumed to benefit from participation, since they share a common interest in improving the service provided. In contrast, others viewed participation as a means of changing the direction of decisions through the exercise of power. Participation would not benefit all groups, since their interests fundamentally conflict, but would act to further the aims of one at the expense of the other. But among the holders of this general view, there was a striking division, for some believed participation would benefit the consumers while others conversely believed that it would benefit the service providers. As in the preceding case, the introduction of participatory measures was advocated or opposed according to the diagnosis of the direction of change and the values of the particular analyst.

This issue of who benefits from the policies stemming from participation schemes is particularly crucial, and therefore deserves some detailed attention. The assumptions on which such divergent conclusions have been reached must be examined and assessed in the light of the foregoing analysis. It can be seen that they vary with respect to both the interests of the participants and the nature of the process in which they are engaged. The first view, that participation improves decision-making for everyone involved, clearly rests on an assumption that their interests — at least with respect to any issues under discussion — are fundamentally aligned. Participation simply enables them to sit down together and work out how best to put their joint concerns into practice. With no conflict (or, in a somewhat modified version, little conflict) there is no real problem for negotiation. Furthermore, the particular methods of participation, the structures established, have little import. As the interests are shared in the first place, the end result of any discussions will be agreeable to all sides.

The second view, that participation brings about decisions in the interests of one group only, rests on highly divergent assumptions.

The interests of the consumers and service-providers are not congruent, but conversely fundamentally in conflict. They can be plotted on a one-dimensional continuum, with consumers at one end and the service-providers at the other, and the results of any discussions, the decisions made, can similarly be so plotted. In simple terms, the more that is done favouring consumers, the less it will favour the service-providers, and vice versa. Participation is not about working together to achieve joint aims, but entails a constant power struggle between the two sides. Consequently, the arrangements for participation, the structures established, matter considerably, for they are assumed to both reflect and determine the distribution of power between consumers and service-providers. They, too, can be plotted on a single continuum, for they affect whose interests are served by decisions, who gets their way in the end.

This case is spelled out in a frequently cited article on citizen participation in planning by Sherry Arnstein. She sets out a 'ladder of participation' from less to more participation, with the following steps: (i) manipulation, (ii) therapy (both seen as 'non-participation'), (iii) informing, (iv) consultation, (v) placation (all seen as 'degrees of tokenism'), (vi) partnership, (vii) delegated power and (viii) citizen control (all seen as 'degrees of citizen power').[18] Many writers have taken this general construct, refined or re-labelled its categories and applied it to other policy areas.[19] It has proved an enormously popular means of depicting the conflicts entailed by participation. It represents a complete contrast from – and indeed a reaction to – the view of participation as a means of furthering jointly held aims.

What is being argued by those accepting this analysis is that particular arrangements for participation produce particular, predictable, results. Two separate explanations are commonly offered for the achievement of these predicted outcomes. First, some suggest that the effects of participation follow closely from the intentions of those responsible for establishing it. Where decision-makers implement participation in order to manipulate consumers or to persuade them to their own point of view, for instance, then the result will be such manipulation or persuasion. Where, in contrast, participation is introduced in order to provide a service more to consumers' liking, then the result will be more consumer-oriented policies. This position is often taken by those who view decision-makers' motives with suspicion, and is used to question the likelihood that participation will further consumers' aims. As Pateman writes, about industrial participation:

That writers on management do not discriminate more carefully between different 'participatory' situations is not surprising when one considers their reason for being interested in participation in the workplace. For them, it is just one management technique among others that may aid the achievement of the over-all goal of the enterprise — organisational efficiency.[20]

Secondly, others argue that the effects of participation can be derived from an examination of the formal structures in which it is embodied. Indeed, such structures may be seen as intervening variables between the intentions of the introducers and its results. In other words, those who wish to increase the power of the consumer will set up structures suitable to this end, and those who wish to limit their power will similarly be guided in the sort of arrangement they establish. The crucial factor is the nature of the powers devolved to the consumer side; where these are considerable, decisions will favour the consumers, and where these are negligible, decisions will favour the service providers. Since most systems for participation do not devolve many formal powers on to consumers (indeed, their complete devolution would entail consumer control, not participation), there is again a tendency for those holding this position to question the likelihood that participation will further consumers' interests.

The problems underlying both these views of participation, that it is a vehicle solely for co-operation on the one hand and solely for conflict on the other, can now be seen clearly. Neither is wholly wrong for, as demonstrated above, consumers and service-providers have some interests which they hold in common and some which they hold alone. Neither, however, is wholly right. The two groups approach each other neither as friendly colleagues nor as hostile adversaries, but as some combination of the two; new alliances and cleavages develop over different issues and over time. Thus, the view that participation acts to benefit both sides, on the assumption that their interests are fully congruent, misses the extent to which there is conflict between them. But equally, the view that participation acts to benefit one group at the expense of the other, on the assumption that their interests are wholly conflicting, misses the extent to which there are common aims between them. Both are partially correct, but by being partial, are fundamentally misleading.

Similarly, the assumption underlying both views that the impact of participation will necessarily be of a particular kind, whether favourable to the consumers, the service providers or both, is un-founded. Of course, those establishing participatory arrangements will have certain goals which they hope to achieve. Indeed, those joining in at a later date will have their goals, and will hope they will be achieved. But there is no means by which either group can ensure that they will get their way. The process of bargaining which participation necessarily entails makes the result of their discussions uncertain and unpredictable.

Nor can the results of participation be assumed to follow from the particular institutional structures established. The consumer partici-pants may be given many or few formal powers, and the extent of these powers may assist or retard their efforts to achieve particular ends. But formal powers are not the same as effective power; they help, but they assure nothing. It is the effective power, the combination of resources which groups mobilise in their cause, which is the critical variable determining who gets what they want in the end. Consequently, the results of participation cannot be predicted on the basis of formal structures alone. Plotting schemes on a continuum or ladder according to their formal structure is not a meaningful exercise. It cannot depict the bargaining power of the groups involved, nor the extent to which some results benefit both sides. In sum, it cannot depict the relative effectiveness of different arrangements with any accuracy.

Again it should be stressed that the analysis of the processes of participation presented here applies most strongly in the context of arrangements for direct participation. Whatever the nature of partici-pation, the results cannot be predicted from the intentions of either side nor from the nature of the formal mechanisms employed. The assumption of overlapping interests similarly holds whether participa-tion is direct or indirect. But when consumers and decision-makers confront each other directly, they have the greatest opportunity to engage in bargaining – to persuade, cajole and win concessions – to gain, in short, some ground. In the absence of such contact, they can try to do so, but their very isolation limits their ability to do so effec-tively.

Once participation is seen as a process entailing bargaining in the context of overlapping interests, the existence of conflicting claims regarding its results becomes understandable. These claims, as noted at the outset of this chapter, are not established fact but simply hypotheses, or expectations, about what participation entails and what it can achieve. The variety of behaviour encompassed by participation, and the variety of results to which it can lead, together enable a number of different expectations to be held at the same time. All make sense before deliberations have begun. With respect to the process of decision-making, for instance, it is quite reasonable to expect the new participants to act as contributors of information, helping the decision-makers to formulate plans more sensibly. It is equally reasonable to expect them to enter into a more active debate in an effort to sway decisions to their own ends. Similarly, with respect to the results of their joint discussions, it is reasonable to expect decisions to be largely favourable to the service-providers, since they may well prove more adept at winning consumers to their own point of view. But equally, it is reasonable to expect decisions to reflect consumers' concerns, since they too may prove successful at demonstrating the cogency of their position. It is in the nature of any bargaining situation that each group will do what it can to move decisions in the direction of its own interests. It is also in the nature of the situation that each may prove successful in some circumstances. While conflicting expectations make no sense after the event, their joint existence can be explained by the indeterminacy of the situation before it.

The impact of participation: some brief comments

One might well ask, however, what factors do affect the nature and direction of the impact of consumer-participation schemes. It has been argued that this cannot be traced simply to the intentions of the introducers or to the particular formal structures established. But it is unlikely to be wholly arbitrary. The effectiveness of consumers, or decision-makers, in these schemes can be seen as a function of the leverage which they can bring to bear on their discussions, and this consists of a host of ostensibly unrelated factors. A few can be identified here.

To a considerable extent, relative effectiveness is based on what might be called simple political clout: the size of the constituency which will be affected by issues, the saliency of the issues for the people involved, the extent to which either group can attain their ends by less-desirable means. All sorts of resources, not least financial, may play a part here, affecting their ability to communicate their views to others and mobilise interests on their behalf. In a slightly different vein, the willingness of either side to listen to the other is also important: the extent to which they share common backgrounds, hold common assumptions, accept each other's legitimacy or approach their discussions in an acceptable style. Both groups will also be affected by their confidence and skills in debate, their ability to express themselves effectively and to penetrate the loyalties of the other side. On a wider front, the general environment in which decisions take place must have some impact, including the economic climate and political developments outside the immediate issue at hand. Finally, the influence of each group will be affected by their respective abilities to manipulate the discussion process itself, to determine what gets on the agenda, to interject relevant information or bring in outside expertise, and to close the debate. This is in itself no small subject; it is the meat and drink of political analysis.

But many may be wondering where, in all this theorising, is any evidence. The accuracy of the many assertions reviewed here, as well as the assumptions underlying them, can only truly be assessed in the light of data on real participation schemes. Does participation affect the participants' fulfilment, or sense of social integration or belief in their political institutions? Does it improve their capacities to deal with the world? Does it enable them to get their way, other things being equal, more often than not? These are the crucial questions and they require results, lots of them, in order to be answered.

There are a number of problems here, which can only be touched on briefly. First, the evidence is surprisingly limited; there simply has not been that much research devoted to these questions. Secondly, and not at all surprisingly in the light of this analysis, what results there are are very mixed. No single view has emerged on these issues, for most of the possible answers have been found in one study or another. But thirdly, and arising directly from the preceding point, there are real problems of interpretation. It is exceedingly difficult to measure fulfilment or developed capabilities or participant influence. And it is equally difficult to *interpret* both cause and effect and the significance of any given findings.

Two examples may help to illustrate this last point. Firstly, one area where there is quite a bit of evidence is the relationship between participation and a heightened sense of efficacy, the *'feeling* that one is capable of influencing the public decision-making process'.[21] A positive association between general political participation and a sense of efficacy has been demonstrated many times over; a recent summary of such studies cites twenty-four separate examples.[22] But while this association can be interpreted to suggest that participation increases efficacy, the causality may also work in the opposite direction – efficacy may increase participation. People's attitudes may be changed by participation, in other words, but those with certain attitudes may be more inclined to participate in the first place. The data are, by themselves, consistent with either view and indeed the causality may work both ways. The important point here is the difficulty of asserting either position with great confidence.

Secondly, there is the problem of assessing influence. Only a few studies have tried to answer the knotty problem of who gains by participation, whose policies win the day. Here, decisions (and even non-decisions) can be studied and some attempt made to determine the extent of participant influence. But interpreting such results is not an easy matter. The decisions may be what the participants wanted, but might they have been taken in exactly the same way without the participants' presence? The decisions may appear to go against what the participants pressed, but were the service-providers' opinions subtly changed in the course of their discussions, to be reflected in subsequent decisions? And what significance can be placed on the results? In his study of tenant consultations, for instance, Saunders argues that they achieved 'a certain degree of success', but then casts doubt on their importance: 'But these are arguably minor victories (concessions is perhaps a more appropriate term), for while the tenants' associations appear to win, nobody seems to lose; i.e. such victories are in no way redistributive.'[23] Indeed, he goes even further. Through participation 'within the system', the tenants are said to have reduced, rather than strengthened, their own political position:

> They have thus confronted the local authority, not as challengers, but as supplicants. Far from representing a challenge to the prevailing pattern of resource allocation, they have strengthened the pattern of distribution by competing for the crumbs while resolutely ignoring the cake.[24]

These assertions may or may not be right; that is not the point. They are included here simply to illustrate the problem of interpretation. Saunders found some gains but translated these into losses; another writer might equally have seen the minor gains as the first step to even greater ones. Results, in other words, are interesting and they are necessary, but they do not altogether solve the problem of understanding the impact of participation. They require interpretation, and interpreting the interpreters.

Summary

By elaborating the many conflicting claims which have been put forward for participation, the preceding chapter set up an analytical puzzle with respect to its results. This chapter has attempted to 'solve' that puzzle by considering the nature of the participatory process. Because it entails bargaining between the new participants and the service-providers, and because their interests are to some extent (but not wholly) overlapping, the outcome of their interaction is not determined from the outset. Many different expectations can reasonably be held about who might gain from the introduction of participation. Even once it has been effected, its impact can prove difficult to assess. Participation, in sum, gives rise to many different interpretations.

The ambiguity attached to participation has, however, helped to foster its own cause. Because so many different hopes have been linked with it, so many different expectations about what it will achieve, it has been embraced by spokesmen of highly varying political hues. Consumers have advocated participation in order to achieve their particular ends and the service-providers have similarly welcomed it in order to serve theirs. The very uncertainty of its impact has enabled a common rallying call. But why should this have come to be so compelling during the past decade? What changes generated this particular response? The following chapter is addressed to these questions.

6 The genesis of participation

Whatever its roots in political philosophy over the centuries, interest in extending the boundaries of participation is essentially a modern, and indeed a recent, phenomenon. In the case of consumer participation in social policy decision-making, it is a subject which has only come to the fore in the past decade or so. Yet, as demonstrated in the preceding chapters, interest has not been limited to a few eccentric advocates nor to a single service. On the contrary, it has spread to all areas of social policy and generated proponents in many different corners of the political spectrum. Participation is an idea whose time had clearly come. The question naturally arises of why this should be so.

To provide an explanation for any widespread social change is no easy task. It is necessary to identify both *who* was responsible for bringing it about and *why* they sought to do so. Where, as in the case of participation, more than one group is associated with the cause, their aims may well be found to differ from one another. Indeed, they may not all be responding to the same basic problem. Thus, it is often argued that participation is something that consumers have themselves demanded, reflecting a growing unwillingness to accept the authority of others to formulate policies on their behalf. But they are only one part of the story. As shown already, demands for their involvement have also stemmed from those responsible for providing services, arising from considerations of both a technical and political nature. Moreover, ostensibly disinterested outsiders have also been active in this area, pressing participation on to the political agenda for a host of disparate reasons. No single group can readily be given sole credit for this change. Equally, no single problem can readily be shown to underlie its advocacy. The job of unravelling the issues and pressures is not an altogether simple one.

The fashionability thesis

What plausible hypotheses, then, can be offered to explain the sudden growth of interest in the idea of participation during the decade or so following the late 1960s? One answer, quite simply, is that it became fashionable, and that its manifestation in so many different areas was the result of the public and policy-makers alike 'jumping on the band-wagon'. Clearly, ideas like participation, which can easily be translated from one context to another, are likely to be picked up and used if they appear to meet a responsive chord. More than many other issues, participation offers an emotive rallying cry, highly useful to politicians searching for a potentially popular cause. Furthermore, few find it easy to oppose it openly.

There is some evidence that fashionability played some part in the spread of participation in some areas. If not the sole explanation, it certainly helped to assist the cause. In the case of the community health councils, for instance, their introduction, as part of the re-organisation of the National Health Service in 1974, has been attributed directly to this impetus. They were not invented by those who would play any part in their operation, but by others (Ministers and civil servants) who viewed them as a convenient way of solving a wider political problem. As Klein and Lewis write:

> And although the plans for reorganisation had begun to evolve in the mid-sixties, the era of interest in planning, they had been completed in the 'seventies, the era of interest in participation. The political problem, therefore, was how to best square the circle of elitism and populism: how to reconcile the emphasis on centralised planning with the currently fashionable rhetoric of local participation.[1]

The introduction of these bodies clearly served this purpose; they demonstrated that consumers had some means of expressing their views on health matters — of participating, if not in decision-making, at least in discussions about the health service.

Nor was health the only area in which the fashion for participation proved a prime contributor to its articulation. In most other fields, the topicality of this idea acted at least as a spur to its development. In arguing for attention to be given to the idea of involving supplementary benefit claimants, David Donnison, then Chairman of the Supplementary Benefits Commission, stated:

> At a time when the health service, the town planners, the schools, the housing authorities — indeed, virtually every public service — are endeavouring to find more effective ways of giving their customers a voice in their development, the supplementary benefits system stands out as an exception to this trend. I believe we must eventually demonstrate that we too are considering how our claimants can be involved in running the service they depend on so heavily.[2]

With any popular trend, there is bound to be a desire among the more forward thinking not to be the odd man out.

But there is a basic flaw in this thesis. Put crudely, it suggests that participation schemes were popular because they were popular, and does not in itself provide an adequate explanation of why they were popular in the first place. Additional hypotheses are required in order to explain why participation was generally a fashionable phenomenon. This thesis may help to explain why *some* arrangements saw the light of day, and the community health councils may well be among these. It should not, however, be viewed as the sole impetus for all participation schemes; they must be traceable at least in part to other causes.

The growth of consumer demands

A more specific explanation for the genesis of interest in participation at this time can be found in the argument that it stemmed directly from pressures from consumers. Participation was not simply a fashion, it was something that consumers were demanding in order to ensure that their voice was heard. It can be argued that the 1960s saw a general awakening of interest in the services provided by the state, and that parents, tenants and other groups became unwilling to sit idly by while decisions were made on their behalf. They joined together, both locally and nationally, to give themselves some clout and proceeded to demand a right to participate in the policy-making process. The introduction of new systems to enable them to do so may simply represent a direct response to these demands.

A number of different explanations can be given for the increased interest in participation at this time, centring around a change in public attitudes to the providers of statutory services and to the services themselves. Some argue that people simply became unwilling to accept professional or managerial authority without question. As Sharpe proposes, 'put in its crudest terms, the general public seems to be much less willing than it was in the past to give those in authority the benefit of the doubt when interests are in conflict.'[3] Over many years there had been a growing tendency to question authority in all its manifestations, not only in the public sphere of government officials but also in more private relationships – the vicar, the doctor, the husband and father. People began to feel more able to argue, to assert their own views, to be more involved. This translated itself into demands for participation in many new areas.

There are, in fact, two separate trends here, both pointing in a single direction. On the one hand, rising educational standards and changes in the occupational structure meant that more people were capable, and equally important *felt* capable, of making many decisions themselves. They had been increasingly trained to think for themselves, to question others, and not unnaturally began to apply their capacities in new directions. On the other hand, people began to take a look at *who* was making decisions for them and were not wholly impressed. Particular policies were no longer seen as inevitable, but 'the result of someone's decision, the decision of an identifiable individual, e.g. the president, the director, or some official'.[4] These were not, perhaps, so expert as had been imagined, but 'fallible human beings like the rest of us, and frequently misinformed and stupid to boot'.[5] In other words, the inequality in the perceived ability of the two sides – professional and client, manager and managed, official and citizen – began to narrow. The mystique formerly attached to professionals and managers, to those who had once been able to take decisions without question, had begun to fade.

But there were also other changes. People's expectations of their services began to change too. It was not simply that those in power did not retain an aura of authority about them, but that they did not deliver the goods. People became more demanding about what they got and about their rights to certain standards. The 'revolution of rising expectations' which had once referred only to the attainment of traditional consumer goods and services began to apply equally to the context of state-provided benefits and services. And in many spheres standards were felt to be falling. Parents became worried about what their children were learning in school; tenants became concerned about increasing vandalism on their council estates. People had begun to expect certain standards, and where they did not get them, to take action to see that they did.

It is, indeed, probable that changing expectations in the two sectors, the private and the public, were not unrelated. As conditions improve in one sphere, it is only natural to look for a corresponding improvement in another. This involves not only things which bring material well-being but also all the other intangibles in life that make people feel at peace with themselves. As Arblaster has argued, the rise in people's living standards had entailed also a rise in their status, but this was not matched by a 'corresponding increase in their power either as citizens or workers'.[6] Together with increased educational levels, this meant that participation was demanded 'as one reaction among others to a widespread dislocation between political and social power on the one hand and social and economic status on the other'.[7] More and more people, in other words, had come to feel that they deserved something better.

It is also probable that demands to participate tend to escalate. Participation is not something that, once achieved, makes people stop wanting it and turn to other issues. Participation, in itself, gives (or at least *may* give) the participator an appetite for more, the desire for more power or for more opportunities in other spheres. Students, for instance,

> were sometimes listened to before they were given seats in university senates, and listened to more systematically afterwards, when they made use of their seats. Some of them have felt, however, that the representation is only token and the participation is less than genuine; so the inclination to demand to participate has recurred.[8]

Participation can politicise the participant consumers and make them more demanding. At least some pressures from consumers can be traced to this desire for more involvement, for attention in new areas of service provision.

Finally, some would argue that there was a sea-change in people's feelings about politics itself, about their respective roles in the public and private spheres. The decade of the 1950s is often characterised as a period of apathy, of withdrawal to the comforts and peace of domestic life. The move toward involvement, so visible from the mid-1960s, can be seen as a direct reaction to the preceding period, a concern to impress one's own perspectives on to the public scene, to get to the centre of things. As Kateb writes:

What is in play is a positive concept of politics, and a corresponding desire to make as many kinds of human relations as possible into political relations. Put negatively, there is a disdain for passivity. There is a repugnance toward being administered, commanded, or manipulated; and not only that, but a repugnance toward being governed; and beyond that, a repugnance toward being represented.[9]

People, under this view, wanted to participate directly, to become — in all senses of the word — involved.

But these are all reasons why consumers may have wished to participate; they do not explain why they achieved any success. To the extent that the introduction of participation can be traced to demands from consumers at all, why should they have been able to make their voice heard in this way? One answer, quite simply, is that there were many more of them. The sheer numbers of people affected by statutory services had been growing and may have reached a crucial level by about this time. Planners had turned their attention not only to specific problem areas within local authorities but also to developing general plans for each authority as a whole, affecting large numbers of new people. Housing authorities had been active in building new dwellings and through 'municipalisation' taking more houses into the public domain. Education had extended downwards to include more pre-school children and upwards through increasing numbers remaining in school longer, not to mention the consumers of various forms of higher education. Because of a growth in the range of welfare benefits, more people found themselves in the role of claimants at some point in their lives. Through all these developments, the number of people whose lives were affected in some way by state policies for social welfare had increased dramatically in the decade or so preceding the period in question.

There was also, however, a much more compelling factor. There were not only more consumers — they became more organised. The periods both pre-dating the interest in participation and coinciding with it witnessed an enormous growth in the number of local associations concerned with specific services. There was a proliferation of tenants' associations, of parents groups, of groups focussed on specific health and social problems and, not least, of both community and amenity associations concerned with particular local areas. This growth was both geographic, with increased coverage of old areas and attention to new ones, and functional, with groups developing for new issues and problems. Nor was it solely a development confined to a single social class. Some, like local tenants' associations, were clearly working class; others, like amenity societies, were largely middle class; others still managed to be a combination of the two. People were busy joining associations to protect their interests and further their particular concerns. Moreover, many national pressure groups were formed at this time around consumer problems, some independent of any local bodies and others acting specifically to co-ordinate their operation and articulate their needs.

These organisations were strengthened by their ability to draw upon consumers' growing experience with the very services in question. The fact that the welfare state had been in existence for some time meant that people had become more familiar with it, and increasingly able to deal with the system. Through joint action, they could bring their collective concerns to public attention and do so effectively because of their familiarity with it. New tenants, after all, know little about housing management, but over the years gain considerable knowledge of how decisions get made. Residents of unplanned areas know little about the planning process, but once their area is the target of change they gain familiarity with the means by which plans get made. New parents do not know how to influence the direction of school policy, but over time can gain considerable insights into what can and cannot be done. Furthermore such knowledge — and the ability to use it — is cumulative. Experience in dealing with housing managers can be fairly readily translated into coping with teachers or headmasters and so forth. The simple longevity of many services may well have acted to breed a more sophisticated and able populace. They turned their growing skills into an important organisational resource.

In passing, it is interesting to speculate about the reasons for the proliferation of organisations devoted to particular consumer causes. What changes brought about an interest in organising around social and community issues? Some would argue that these organisations arose because of the sheer numbers of people affected by statutory services. They became increasingly visible to one another, both because of their numbers and because they came into increasing contact with one another, and this stimulated them to join together into formal or informal groups. From casual meetings in the health centre or school or housing estate, they began to talk to one another about their problems and to propose collective action to do something about them.

But the existence of large numbers, even in close proximity, is not a sufficient basis for explaining a tendency to organise. What additional incentives were at play? One answer is that they were mobilised by outsiders — various social and community workers who saw in their organisation one means of helping consumers to get the services they needed or wanted. Indeed, many workers were paid to do just this, and many groups undoubtedly owed their existence to their efforts. But many others also formed spontaneously, without any external assistance. It can be argued that the very forces that made people want to participate in decision-making spurred them also to join associations, both to help them 'take on' the system and as a source of interest in its own right. Their very questioning of authority, their very insistence on high standards, and their search for a new kind of politics may have acted as an impetus both to form new groups and join existing ones.

It can equally be argued, however, that the causation was not one-way. Many groups may have been formed in order to try to attain a certain level of services, but the very level of services itself may have acted to stimulate consumer organisation. The sophistication bred of many years' experience with the system may have spurred an interest in joint action to get their way. Indeed, exactly because the state provided so much, consumers had more to gain from organising, and more to lose from not doing so. It is not simply that there were more consumers, and that they were more willing and able to confront the service-providers; they had a growing incentive to ensure that their voice was heard.

Whatever the reasons for the growth of consumer organisations, it is clear that they did proliferate at this time and that among the other issues which they raised, participation was a common call. Educational groups, both nationally and locally, pressed for greater parental repre-sentation on governing boards. Housing groups, again both nationally and locally, pressed for tenant participation in council housing manage-ment. Local community groups, both tenants and residents associations and amenity societies, regularly pursued the cause of greater participa-tion in local planning decisions. And, of course, many were highly successful, gaining both local arrangements for consultation and national commitment to the cause, even legislation. Some commen-tators ascribe to these groups the principal credit for institutional changes. It has been argued, for instance, that the whole concept of public participation,

arose primarily from the burgeoning self-help groups in social welfare and education. These movements were associated with the growing concern of left-wing politics with community issues, housing and services. Grass roots activity continuously threw into relief the need for a fresh approach to social and environmental issues.[10]

One must be cautious, however, in attributing too much influence to these consumer groups. It is true that they grew in number and it is also true that most advocated greater participation in policy-making in their respective sphere. It does not follow, however, that the introduction of measures for participation derived directly from their calls. They were not only not the sole influence on decision-makers at this time but also did not always have their ear at all. It is necessary to explore what other considerations affected decisions on this question.

The needs of the service-providers

One of the more striking changes in service-provision, introduced exactly during the period in question, was a dramatic growth in the scale of the institutions through which services were administered and delivered. Not only did individual authorities become larger, but many individual institutions also grew in size, so that new administrative layers tended to be created between those who determined policies and those for whom services were provided. It can be argued that this trend, more than pressures from consumers as such, played the key role in the development of participatory mechanisms because of the problems it engendered for the service-providers themselves. A very considerable gulf emerged between them and their clientele, and they wanted new ways of re-bridging the gap. They sought the participation of consumers, it can be suggested, as a response to their own political and professional needs for contact with them.

It might seem odd to suggest that those who are responsible for providing state services have any need for regular interaction with their consumers. From their point of view, it might be thought altogether simpler to get on with the business of making decisions without any interference from the outside world. But that is not, in fact, how either politicians or professionals tend to operate. Local authority councillors, for instance, must submit themselves for re-election on a regular basis and to be successful they need, quite simply, votes. While those in some constituencies may have few worries in this respect, most members will feel they need the ear of their electorate, to demonstrate their efforts on voters' behalf and learn what issues are worrying them. They need to be able to talk on a regular basis with people who know the public mood.

The situation with officials is not so different. They, too, need to know what is publicly acceptable in order to advise the politicians in a sensitive manner. They may also have their own professional reasons for wanting to feel the collective pulse of their particular consumers, however. To a large extent this derives from what they are taught is good professional practice. In the case of housing, for instance, 'good management' is said to require 'the application of skill . . . in developing a sound relationship between landlord and tenants . . . in order that the estate, as well as the individual houses, may give the fullest value to both the landlord and the tenants.'[11] Such a 'sound relationship' is also sought in many other professional circles — doctors with their patients, teachers with their pupils' parents, social workers with their clients and so forth. It is part of what being a good professional is about.

This desire for good relations can be expressed in many different ways and interpreted in many different lights. For some, it is clearly one aspect of well-meaning paternalism. Octavia Hill, for example, seen as the 'originator of modern principles of enlightened housing management'[12] said of her tenants that it was necessary 'to endeavour to be so unfailingly just and patient that they should learn to trust the rule that was over them'.[13] For others, it is simply an obvious adjunct to carrying out professional tasks, as in this later writing on the same subject: 'the regular and friendly contact between manager and tenant by which this relationship [of mutual responsibility] would be established provides the manager with that knowledge of the tenants and their circumstances which is essential for her work.'[14] Contact may be sought in order to increase the flow of information and ideas upwards, as argued by the former Chairman of the Supplementary Benefits Commission 'we must be willing to listen to the views of those who depend on us for their livelihoods for we have much to learn from them.'[15] Alternatively, it may be sought in order to increase the flow in the opposite direction, as argued by one planner with respect to the public: 'town planners . . . will have to be trained not only in their professions but also as public speakers and become skilled in the art of persuasion.'[16]

The point is that, whatever the complexity of the reasoning underlying its advocacy, professionals in most fields seek some means of
keeping their ear to the ground of their particular clientele. They may
want to preach, they may want to learn, they may want to convince
themselves that they have the full approval or general trust of their
clients or claimants or the public at large. They may well wish to do
all of these things. What they require is some means of interaction with
the relevant groups on a formal or informal basis. The development of
systems of public participation clearly serves this very distinctive purpose.

If participation was so much in the service-providers' interest, one
may ask, why was it not introduced much earlier? The answer is that
while these aims have not changed much over time, the ability to
realise them has changed very considerably. In the case of housing, for
example, the change in the scale of the activity of management has had
a dramatic effect on the ease of contact between senior managers and
tenants. When the stock of housing managed by authorities was relatively small, there was no need to formalise their interaction, for
tenants and officers could meet regularly on an informal basis to discuss matters of concern to either group; even senior officers could be
available for consultation as required. But as councils constructed and
acquired increasing numbers of dwellings, the housing departments
administering these dwellings inevitably grew. There were not only
more staff employed but also greater specialisation, both on a functional and on a geographical basis. The net effect was a growing gap
between the tenants on the one hand and the officers making broad
policy decisions on the other. Some departments attempted to overcome this problem by employing large numbers of on-the-ground
personnel, but these only served to enlarge the number of personnel
levels between tenants and senior staff.

This dilemma is aptly described by a text published in 1959, at just
the time that many housing departments were growing due to the
growth of their council housing stock:

> The housing manager to a public authority acts as their link with
> their individual tenants, and has the task of encouraging mutual
> understanding and consideration and seeing that the responsibilities
> of both landlord and tenant are carried out. . . .
>   The housing manager in charge of a small estate will know all
> the tenants and their families. As the number of lettings increases,

he will require assistance but will still expect to know the tenants personally and to be fully conversant with general matters. . . .

The housing manager (in a large office) cannot personally know thousands of tenants and their families though he should be careful not to become too inaccessible to them. He must rely increasingly on assistants who will carry out the greater part of interviewing, visiting and correspondence with tenants. . . . He can no longer, as in a small office, have continuous direct contact with all his staff, and much information has to filter up, and down, through senior staff.[17]

Regular meetings between senior housing managers and their junior staff were encouraged since 'those who make the final decisions in an executive capacity tend to be remote from the people affected by the decisions'[18] and meetings with tenant associations were likewise urged.[19]

The following two decades only served to exacerbate the problem so clearly described by this text. Regular contact between senior officials and tenants became increasingly difficult to attain as local authority tenants grew in numbers. Not only had there been a period of active housing construction, but two local government reorganisations (in 1965 in London and in 1974 in the rest of the country) meant that large housing stocks were created through the amalgamation of smaller authorities into larger ones. In London, indeed, the housing owned by individual boroughs also grew following the handover of many estates formerly owned by the Greater London Council in the early 1970s. The introduction of tenant participation schemes at this time can be seen as a response by housing managers to the problem of maintaining regular contact with tenants, which had been achieved by more informal means in earlier years.

The growth of administrative units was not, however, confined to the housing field. During the decade or so from 1965 there was a notable trend toward amalgamation and centralisation in the administration and delivery of virtually all the public welfare services in Britain. This occurred at two levels. At the point of delivery — the individual school, hospital or health centre — the tendency toward larger institutions simply continued. At the point of overall policy-making — the authority responsible for administering the services in question — the change was much more dramatic. Under a wave of enthusiasm for greater management efficiency, vast changes were introduced in the systems by which services were administered within both central and local government.

The most comprehensive change during the period in question was the reorganisation of local government in 1974. It meant that nearly 1,400 local authorities outside London were reduced to just over 400, with similar changes having been effected in the Greater London area in 1965. The result of these changes was that each local government department had to deal with a large administrative area and each councillor to speak for a larger number of constituents. Many services were affected directly. The number of schools for which each education authority was responsible grew; the number of houses each housing authority had to manage grew; the size of areas to be planned by individual sets of planners grew. And with the increased scale of provision, the administrative units established to run these services also grew. Increasing layers of officials had to be created to mediate between those on the ground and those making decisions at the top of the hierarchy. Nor was the tendency to amalgamation solely geographic. The early 1970s also saw the creation of new social services departments from what had been separate children's, welfare and health departments. These changes also entailed more administrative layers between policy-makers and consumers.

Similar developments also occurred in central government. The National Health Service reorganisation in 1974 amalgamated virtually all health delivery systems — hospitals, family practitioners and services previously run by local authorities — into one vast organisation. It, too, resulted in more administrative tiers, and more administrators, than had existed previously. The other side of the Department of Health and Social Security, the former Ministry of Social Security, had been formed in 1966 from two separate agencies, combining two entirely separate benefit systems into one. The local offices administering these benefits were also increasingly merged, creating larger units of administration.

One significant effect of all these management changes, whatever the increased efficiency with which the services were run, was to isolate the policy-makers from those who had to bear the consequences of their decisions. Chief officers found themselves not only with increased responsibilities but also with increased administrative layers between themselves and the consumers of their services. Local authority councillors, too, had to cover larger geographic areas and familiarise themselves with a wider range of problems. For the reasons already explored, many found this an unsatisfactory way of running things. They needed some way to regain some contact with their consumers, preferably representative ones, to discuss their service provision. Participation seemed an obvious answer.

There is no doubt that at least some schemes for consumer participation derived directly from this impetus. Most patient participation groups, for instance, were started by doctors, often in health centres, concerned to secure greater familiarity with patients' needs and problems. As one general practitioner, active in starting a group, wrote about its value: 'This should benefit patients; it certainly benefits doctors and staff by giving them more confidence in managing the service. They know they have their patients' support — *because they have asked them*.'[20] Similarly, most tenant participation schemes set up in the early 1970s were instigated by housing officers and councillors, anxious to increase their communication with tenants. As one advocate stated: 'What better aid to management is there than to have a formal and frequent method of allowing tenants to individually and collectively voice their opinions, needs, and preferences?'[21] Participation was not simply something which was in the air; it had explicit benefits for the service-providers, legitimising their decisions not only in consumers' eyes but in their own.

That participation was sought by various service-providers (as well as by consumers) is not in question. What is less clear is the underlying reason for their advocacy. Some have argued that they were primarily concerned to protect their professional or political interests, to use the mechanisms of consultation to their own advantage. Sharpe, for instance, argues that planners viewed the new procedures for public participation in planning 'as a gift offering to win back the waning support of the general public and so safeguard the future of planning as a public service'.[22] Goldsmith offers a fuller assessment of their reasoning:

> Thus planners felt that if people could be enabled to understand planning problems and their solutions, and offer their support for what the planners proposed, then objections to proposals would vanish, the process would be speeded up, and blight would be either avoided or minimised. This would be planning by consensus — though apparently a consensus based on what planners felt was the 'best solution' to planning problems.[23]

Involving parents in the running of their schools has been given an even greater role by one commentator:

Parents have been offered the semblance of greater rights over their children's education, on the premise that this would encourage them to press for improvements in educational standards and hence in the conditions for the reproduction of capitalism. So parents have been explicitly used to help solve the current crisis in capitalism.[24]

Summary and discussion

It can be seen that there is no shortage of explanations for the widespread introduction of participation arrangements during the period in question. Consumers had become more demanding, more able, more numerous and, not least, more organised. Concomitantly they began to press for a greater voice in the decision-making process. At the same time, because of changes in the scale of service-provision, policy-makers had become more divorced from the very people for whom their policies were framed, and more frequently criticised for not taking their views into account, They, too, began to seek some contact with their consumers. Furthermore, participation became fashionable, not only in Britain but also, even earlier and fuelling the growing interest, on the other side of the Atlantic. There was a striking convergence of developments during a short space of time, providing a formidable array of pressures towards the implementation of this one idea.

There is no need to calculate exactly the relative roles played by these assorted forces, as they all pulled in the same direction. Indeed, it would not be easy to do so. Participation is the kind of emotive issue for which many different groups tend to want to claim credit. Efforts to disentangle the genesis of any individual participation scheme can quickly run into difficulties. Few people are ever willing to admit their opposition to the idea and many claim responsibility for it when in fact they only responded to initiatives from others. Moreover, on a deeper level, those directly involved are not always aware of the underlying reasons for their interest; they can articulate their public stance but not the broader issues to which they were responding. This means that all discussion of this issue is inevitably partly speculation. Understanding the growth of interest in participation as a general phenomenon presents the same problems writ large.

What can be noted in this development, however, is the wide range of reasoning which was apparently brought to bear on this one issue. Both consumers and service-providers may have been active in welcoming participatory arrangements, but they did not all do so with the same ends in mind. Those on the receiving end of services were largely concerned to get their views taken into account when decisions were being made for them. They wanted to ensure certain standards in their schools, keep their estates properly maintained, limit drastic changes in their neighbourhood and so forth. Some had tried to do so individually over the years, but concluded that through collective action on an official basis they might be able to do so more effectively. They saw participation, in short, as a means of getting things done.

The motivations of the service-providers were undoubtedly more complex. Some were concerned to listen to their consumers and, where appropriate, to modify plans in accordance with their views. Others wanted to assure themselves that they had the confidence of those for whom decisions were made, that the policies they would implement anyway were the right ones for their audience. Still others wanted to persuade that audience that this was so, to set out the constraints affecting them and thereby demonstrate the need for particular courses of action. Most professionals, whether planners or housing managers or social workers, want to carry their clientele with them, to establish and maintain good relations with their respective publics. Most politicians, for more easily identifiable reasons, also want to keep a close watch on their constituents' collective pulse. Participation, in the views of these decision-makers, is a means of fostering mutual understanding.

All of these aspirations are, of course, wholly familiar. Expressed in another way, they represent the various claims for (and against) participation set out in Chapter 4. It can come as no surprise that people pressed for participation for different reasons or held different assumptions about what it would achieve. Consumer participation, it must be reiterated, simply means the introduction of a new group of people, some consumers, into the decision-making process. There is a wide range of purposes in getting them there. What they actually do there is, furthermore, another matter.

The implementation of consumer participation can be seen as, in itself, a kind of institutional bargain between service-providers and consumers, albeit one rarely viewed explicitly in this way. Both parties expect to gain some benefits from its existence. Consumers achieve a formalised voice in the decision-making process, the possibility of exerting some real influence over policies which affect them. Decision-makers gain an increased legitimacy for their decisions, the ability to assert with confidence that they have listened to consumers' views.

Moreover, individual consumers, as well as individual service-providers, stand to gain from their involvement, extending their experience to a new range of problems and consequently increasing their own political resources. The widespread implementation of participation offers visible evidence of the attractiveness of this bargain in many quarters.

7 Some concluding comments

The present scene

Participation in social policy, as defined and discussed in this analysis, no longer engenders the enthusiasm that it once enjoyed. There are occasional articles on the subject in professional journals, but the once-heavy flow of exhortation has diminished to a trickle. There is the occasional conference to discuss its benefits in selected subject areas, but the once frequent meetings to pass on the latest developments have turned instead to new problems. The issue is no longer in the air, on people's minds, a matter of any urgency. It is largely off the political agenda.

There are a number of reasons for this change. To some extent it may be attributed to the swings of fashion, which function in the world of ideas, along with the world of clothes and holiday resorts, more regularly than is often appreciated. Participation was brought to public attention in the late 1960s, and remained a prominent subject for concern for at least a decade. It had a good running, a lot of attention, but it is hardly surprising if new issues are now supplanting it. And, like other fashions, it may well return.

But there are particular reasons why attention has been diverted in the social policy sphere. The pressures of inflation, of unemployment, and of new measures for dealing with them have all brought in their wake a concentration on more immediate problems. At a time when those responsible for managing the social services are searching anxiously for means of conserving their resources, it is not to be expected that they would be excessively concerned about any measures which might add to existing calls on them. Consumers of state services themselves have also been put on the defensive, attempting to preserve

117

their benefits and services from planned or unplanned erosion. In the midst of these economic demands, no one has had much time to worry about the niceties of how decisions get made.

A third reason for the diminished attention to the issue of participation is the very fact that it has been quietly implemented in many corners of the social policy scene. As explored in Chapter 3, planners have incorporated some techniques of public participation into their everyday work, school governing boards have sprung parent members, community health councils have been established and defended, and so on. The excitement which surrounded the *idea* of participation a decade ago has been somewhat dulled by the sheer success it has achieved in being translated into practice.

Why this should be so is not altogether clear. It must be presumed that the campaigns mounted to press for change generate a certain momentum which cannot be sustained over time. At their height, they invite the proliferation of rhetoric, the elaboration of unconfirmable hopes, about the benefits which the desired change will achieve. Such pronouncements bring in their wake a renewed fervour from the other side, a concern to counter each assertion with an opposing point of view, the declaration of costs in implementing any relevant proposal. Once change has been introduced, and its effects not immediately clear, however, neither those who pressed for it nor those who opposed it can make such claims without fear of contradiction. The day-to-day workings of the institutions for participation are not nearly so exciting as the ideals surrounding their advocacy, and subjecting them to detailed study has little glamour at all. It becomes easier to avoid the subject altogether, to turn to other matters.

In any case, for whatever reason, interest in the mechanisms of consumer participation has considerably diminished. On the other hand, it has by no means dried up entirely. Two separate acts of parliament, mandating a measure of consumer participation in education and housing respectively, were passed as recently as 1980. The successful defence of the community health councils, under threat of abolition for well over a year, was achieved only in 1981. Also in the sphere of health, professional interest in and enthusiasm for patients' participation groups appeared to mount during 1981-82. It has not been an entirely dormant period for the cause of participation.

Furthermore, new waves of interest in this general subject have begun to develop at this time, but are expressed in different ways. The emergence of the Social Democratic Party was partly fuelled by concern over exactly such issues as the need to foster greater participation. Their interest lies not so much with consumer involvement in social-policy questions, affecting after all only a minority of the general population, but with general public participation and, to some extent, worker participation in the industrial context. As Shirley Williams writes:

> Decentralisation and participation are conducive to greater individual liberty and to fraternity because they restore to people their wholeness; they become . . . members of society in all its aspects, instead of being merely economic instruments of the production process.[1]

Nor are the spokesmen of the centre the only group actively pursuing greater participation. Champions of the 'left' have also begun to give it greater attention:

> We would like to see local communities invited now to share in strategic decision-making over housing, social services and other plans, and then to be engaged (at a neighbourhood level) in the delivery and management of services and more local decisions. . . . Our general principle is that all public services — including the police, social security, gas and electricity boards, and water undertakings — should be decentralised and democratised.[2]

Indeed, the 'right', too, has turned its attention to participation within certain limited contexts such as local voluntary groups. A Conservative spokesman, for instance, recently argued for more community involvement in the delivery of care:

> There can be few people today who believe that it could ever be possible or right for the agencies of the state to have a monopoly in caring. The sharing of responsibility is plain good sense. It is economical; it is flexible; and it invites participation. The last is important at a time when the acceptability and the effectiveness of some forms of care are increasingly questioned.[3]

Some recurrent themes

For all these reasons, then, participation will never pass wholly from the political agenda. The particular manifestations receiving current attention will change over time, but the themes underlying its advocacy will re-surface in largely similar ways. Indeed, this can best be demonstrated by a brief review of the issues raised in discussions of participation in areas not covered by the preceding chapters. The territory looks surprisingly familiar.

In terms of sheer quantity of writings, the subject which has received the greatest attention is the very broad one of general political participation. The nature of democracy, and the degree of citizen participation necessary to sustain it, are issues which have been debated over the centuries, forming a substantial core of the literature of political theory. But interest in this subject became pronounced in the 1950s and 1960s, giving rise to an enormous volume of writings of both a normative and an empirical nature. Publication of new contributions continues to the present, of course, and is unlikely to cease altogether, but as in the case of consumer participation in social policy, attention appears to be turning elsewhere.[4]

Several issues concern writers in this area, but central among them is the extent to which a high level of participation in the ordinary institutions of democracy, such as the electoral process, is desirable. And central to this particular debate is the simple question of the grounds on which such an assessment should be made. While many writers have ostensibly focussed on the extent to which a high level of participation is *feasible*, and others on what an appropriate *definition* of democracy should contain, underlying their attention is this basic issue of what the institutions of democracy should be aiming to achieve.

Many of the early contributors to this debate, arguing that full participation should not necessarily be sought, stressed the goal of political stability. Some participation was deemed to be vital, of course, in order to protect the electorate from arbitrary decisions by political leaders, but too much might lead to ill-considered policies or even totalitarianism. The institutions of democracy were seen primarily as mechanisms for choosing between different sets of decision-makers, and thereby affecting the direction which decisions would take. Here, for instance is the classic definition of democracy offered by Schumpeter: 'that institutional arrangement for arriving at political decisions in which individuals acquire the power to decide by means of a competitive struggle for the people's vote'.[5] And, here is Dahl, stressing the importance of citizen influence: 'Democratic theory is concerned with processes by which ordinary citizens exert a relatively high degree of control over leaders.'[6]

Subsequent writers argued that this view of democracy was too narrow, for it showed no interest in the effects of taking part on the individuals involved. Democracy should be viewed not only as a means of affecting decisions but also, and possibly more importantly, as a way of developing the capacities and sense of self-realisation of individual citizens. Full participation, then, was given pride of place by these writers, since only by becoming involved could such effects be achieved. Here, for instance, are the words of Bachrach, one proponent of this view:

> Defenders of representative democracy persist in posing the wrong question. The fundamental issue is not whether the few rule in the interest of the many or in their own interest. It is rather that they rule and thereby deprive the many of their freedom.[7]

And here is Pateman, yet another advocate of participation:

> The justification for a democratic system in the participatory theory of democracy rests primarily on the human results that accrue from the participatory process. One might characterise the participatory model as one where maximum input (participation) is required and where output includes not just policies (decisions) but also the development of the social and political capacities of each individual, so there is 'feedback' from output to input.[8]

But these arguments are old friends. While those pressing for more consumer participation rarely present these views as direct alternatives, both have been amply demonstrated in that context. Direct participation in issues of social policy is advocated both in order to influence the direction of decisions and to develop the capacities of those involved. The basic issues and themes are exactly the same.

Similar discussions arise in the context of worker participation in industry. This is, again, a subject which has re-surfaced for public attention from time to time, most recently with the publication of the Bullock Report on industrial democracy in 1977.[9] A considerable amount of debate has focussed on ostensibly technical questions — the mechanisms by which employees should be enabled to take part in management. But a great deal of attention has also been given to what such participation achieves. Again, there are those who argue primarily in terms of the immediate interests of the workers so involved:

> The participating worker is an involved worker, for his job becomes an extension of himself and by his decisions he is creating his work, modifying and regulating it. As he is more involved in his work, he becomes more committed to it, and, being more committed, he naturally derives more satisfaction from it.[10]

And, again, there are those who give equal (or greater) attention to the efficiency of the enterprise: 'The technical quality of a decision can be improved if employees with the relevant skills contribute to that decision.'[11] Furthermore, there are those who contend that workers' interests will not be served by participation, that their views will not be better reflected in decisions because they will be co-opted by management:

> Industrial democracy proposals are likely to have the opposite of their supposed effect. That is, most schemes for industrial democracy will involve an absorption of workers' representatives into capitalist forms of control, not a transcending of these. . . . Collective bargaining and worker participation are means by which employers may preserve and consolidate their existing partial degree of control.[12]

Once again, these are not new or surprising positions. The whole issue of who gains by participation, and therefore whether it should be pursued or fought, underlies discussions on industrial democracy in just the same terms as those on consumer participation in social policy. Indeed, the parallels go much further than demonstrated by this brief summary; with workers, as with consumers, such problems are raised as their competence on technical issues, their willingness to take part and their ability to be representative of their wider constituencies.

The principal point to emerge from this very brief review of participation in other spheres is that the subject does not change substantially either between different contexts or over time. The problems of participation remain the same whether one is discussing tenants and housing management, teachers and boards of governors, workers and industrial democracy or the general public and the democratic state. There is little new under the sun. This is a delightful discovery, for it means that the intellectual baggage one has acquired to understand participation in one area can be readily used again in another. It is not necessary to start afresh, to re-think everything from the beginning. Furthermore, whatever the future holds, whatever the new areas in which participation is advocated, the pros and cons will be already known. They must still be applied — and applied with considerable care — to the new context, but a lot of the work has been conveniently done.

Evaluating participation

So, participation is likely to be a matter for discussion, in one context or another, for many years to come. And, in the final analysis, the key question will remain — is it a good thing? Should greater participation — of consumers or workers, in action or decision-making, by direct or indirect means — be encouraged? Under what circumstances? And what is the right amount?

This book has not been devoted to the cause of proselytisation, and there is no intention of starting here. The author's opinions, such as they are, should have no greater bearing on these questions than those of the individual reader. But this does not mean that some help cannot be given toward answering them, a review of the pertinent considerations. It is with this task that this analysis is concluded.

There are two sets of issues which must be addressed in order to determine whether participation is 'a good thing'. First, it is necessary to establish what it actually achieves. Many different claims have been made in this respect, but none has passed into the realm of even broadly accepted fact. To a large extent this derives from sheer lack of appropriate research; few empirical studies have tried to ask, much less answer, the question of what the effects of participation are. But this fact in itself stems from the considerable difficulties which are necessarily encountered in any attempt to study participation in practice. As discussed in Chapter 5, these involve problems both of measurement and of interpretation.

With respect to the developmental impact on the individuals involved, it is no simple matter to devise indicators of the many changes which participation is supposed to effect. It is not easy to measure human fulfilment, or developed capacities, or individuals' sense of social integration or the legitimacy they ascribe to those in positions of authority. It is possible to ask them about all these issues, and to compare the answers either with those of other non-participators or with those of the same group before they became involved. But neither exercise is easily accomplished, and both entail a considerable measure of over-simplification. The results would, rightly, be likely to be treated with some scepticism. Furthermore, even where such measurements were made and some changes noted, it cannot be assumed that they derive from participation as such, for they may be the results of other influences altogether. Or, and this is a considerable theoretical problem, the causation may be seen to work the other way. It has been shown, for instance, that a correlation between participation and a sense of efficacy may arise because participation leads to greater efficacy or because those with a sense of efficacy tend to participate.[13] The same problem arises in the case of people who are fulfilled, or well-integrated into society, or who believe the political system to be legitimate.

With respect to the decisions arising from participation schemes, it is again not entirely easy to trace the effects of the consumer participants on them. Although decisions are more readily identifiable in principle, especially in comparison to changes in the development of the individuals involved, there are a number of factors which inhibit the attribution of consumer influence. Of particular concern is the problem of non-decisions, the issues which never reach the relevant agenda because certain groups want to avoid discussion of them. These are not easily studied, although attempts can be made to do so. But even confining attention to actual decisions, various problems of interpretation arise. First, it is inherently difficult to trace the impact of a single group, the consumers, on the decisions eventually taken; the others involved may argue that the same conclusions would have been reached in their absence. Secondly, in a similar vein, there is the problem of anticipated reactions; the decisions taken may reflect efforts to anticipate the concerns of the new participants, without directly deriving from their involvement. Thirdly, the views of the respective participants about the appropriate course to be taken may change as a result of their discussions, so that particular decisions which would have been opposed *ex ante* are welcomed *ex post*. In other words, people's perceptions of their own interests change, making it difficult to assess who has had any influence on whom. Finally, there are the various ways in which decisions taken may be subverted in the course of their translation into practice; indeed, they may never be implemented at all.

But there is also a much deeper problem to be faced. As explored at length in Chapter 5, the outcomes of participatory discussions are fundamentally unpredictable and therefore not amenable to conclusive analysis. Individual discussions, of course, eventually reach some outcome, and such outcomes can themselves be studied. But no inference can be drawn that the same result will occur elsewhere, even under roughly similar conditions. The introduction of new participants into a debate is not like the introduction of sugar into water or alcohol into the bloodstream. There are no set properties, no known reaction, which will occur every time. The problem is not simply that it cannot be predicted with any degree of accuracy; there is — and there can be — no general theory about what will occur at all. One can only amass evidence and make cautious judgments based upon it.

Researching participation, then, is no easy matter. It is beset with problems of both a technical and an interpretive nature. This is not to argue, however, that it should not be undertaken. If there is to be any evidence with which to assess the impact of participation, some studies must be carried out. Individual schemes should be examined and their results assessed. The various individuals involved in them can be interviewed, the decisions taken can be analysed, and some measure of their impact thereby developed. There is a need for greater information about outcomes, and what people feel about them, in order to understand what participation means in practice.

Deciding what participation does, however, is only the first step towards its evaluation. The second is to determine the weight to be given to particular outcomes. It is not enough to identify its achievements, whatever these are; it is necessary also to decide whether these are desirable, and at what cost. Participation may be found to lead to a greater sense of efficacy among those who participate, for instance, but this does not automatically make it a desired policy prescription. One must decide whether their development in this way is a particularly deserving cause, and balance this against various other effects participation may have. Even from the point of view of one single group, such as the direct participants, it is quite conceivable that participation helps them in one way (by bringing a sense of fulfilment, say) and harms them in another (by increasing their acquiescence to policies not in their interest, say). When more groups' interests are taken into account, the calculation becomes very messy indeed.

None the less, if a definite stance is to be taken on this issue at all, some judgment must be ventured. There are various ways in which this problem might be approached. By far the most common means of assessing any phenomenon is to determine *whose* interests should be paramount and judge it according to the extent to which it furthers their cause. It may be decided that all consumers are the relevant reference group, or all taxpayers or all those who must run social services, or any subset of these or some other group altogether. One must be careful, however, not to equate the interests of *all* groups, or even certain sets of groups, with one another. Council tenants and local authority manual workers may all be 'working class', for example, but their interests in housing management are not identical. Teachers, educational administrators and councillors on the education committee may all 'provide' education, but their interests in educational issues are likewise not identical. Whatever the group chosen, and whatever the reason, the available evidence can then be considered to determine whether participation is in that group's interests. This may not automatically result in agreement among those of a given persuasion. It has already been shown, for instance, that some claim participation to be *in* consumers' interests and others claim it to be *against* them. But some view should, in principle, be reached.

Yet if, as posited earlier in this analysis, the interests of consumers and decision-makers are not wholly in conflict, it might alternatively be argued that participation is desirable because it can benefit both groups at the same time. Particularly in the case of direct participation, the process of discussion and negotiation between the participants facilitates the development of decisions likely to prove more acceptable to all sides. In other words, the bargaining process can be seen as a socially desirable means of reaching the accommodation of seemingly incompatible interests; the solutions, or bargains, reached as a result of it are better from all points of view. Furthermore, some would argue, it is exactly through the pressures and counter-pressures of political debate that a real understanding of the interests involved can be achieved. Introducing a new set of concerned participants into decision-making is, it may be contended, wholly beneficial.

Not everyone would agree with the policy prescription stemming from this analysis, however. First, some would argue that it ignores the important dimension of bargaining power; it is not enough to create a forum for discussions between opposing sides and then assume that the best man will win. Because bargaining resources are unevenly distributed, it is simply the most powerful, rather than the most deserving, who will win the day. Participation, under this view, does not benefit everyone, and certainly not according to any measure of equity. This position may be held both by defenders of consumers' interests, on the grounds that they would be the ones to lose out, and by those concerned to protect the existing system from consumers' demands, on the grounds that they would prove too powerful.

Secondly, some would argue that the advocacy of participation on the basis that everyone benefits is shortsighted because it does not take into account the new participants' long-term interests. While certain decisions would ostensibly be improved as a result of discussion and negotiation, these would not be fundamental ones in terms of consumers' broader goals. Participation may bring about some concessions, even highly beneficial ones, but it is not therefore to be readily embraced. On the contrary, inasmuch as it serves to ameliorate consumers' conditions and soften their resolve to fight on more important issues, it acts against their underlying interests. Mutual short-term gain, in other words, is an insufficient goal.

Thirdly, others would reach the same conclusion but for different reasons. While participation may benefit all the parties involved, not all relevant people are privy to the exercise. For some, the problem here is that those who participate are likely to be unrepresentative of the very population for whom they are supposed to speak. The coverage may be arbitrary or it may be systematically biassed, for instance in favour of the better off and more articulate. In either case, the decisions reached are likely to have some benefit for the involved, but at the expense of those who are excluded. Indeed, the uninvolved may be doubly hampered because the existence of participatory arrangements *appears* to give them a fair hearing.

Others, equally concerned with the problem of the uninvolved, would argue that the service consumers and providers, even if properly represented, do not comprise the total of the relevant population. The two groups may happily increase spending on a particular service, for example, but at the expense of the ordinary taxpayer. This point is more commonly made in discussions of worker participation, where it is suggested that companies have more interests to serve than those of their own employees. Indeed, it is most frequently made in the context of the public sector, with the argument that public bodies should respond to the 'public' interest and not to the private interests of those who work for them. But the exact same arguments hold in the case of consumers, whose private interests cannot be equated with the public at large.

Evaluating participation, then, is not a straightforward matter. Different conclusions may, indeed, be reached in different contexts. One should want to know who the participants are and for whom they speak. To what extent are they representative of their ostensible constituency or of all those who might be affected by the issues at hand? To whom do they listen and to whom do they report? Are most interests represented in fact even if not by a strict interpretation of the participants' route to selection? One should also want to assess the nature of the questions under discussion. Who do they affect? What information is necessary in order to respond to them? How much expertise or interpretation do they require? Furthermore, what is the cost of setting up arrangements for participation? Are new participants easily accommodated into the existing decision-making system? What side-effects will they have on other institutional arrangements and existing informal relationships?

Someone, or more properly a whole host of someones, must make decisions about social policy — about what to do and how to do it — and see that whatever it is in fact gets done. Decision-makers rarely have a mandate on particular issues; they have to decide, as best they can, what is the appropriate course. The central question for evaluating participation is do they do this so much better on their own, unencumbered by the presence of spokesmen for the consumers or workers or the 'community' at large? Is the answer, simply, it depends on *who* is doing the participating, and, even more basically, *what* they decide?

Here is the fundamental dilemma. Most people readily welcome the introduction of participation when the results which emerge — whether particular decisions or even more general changes in attitudes and perspectives — are what they wanted anyway. It is argued that tenants or patients or workers should be able to have their say, but what is really wanted is that they should put into practice certain policies or be helped to come around to a particular point of view. But what happens when the results go the 'wrong' way? How many advocates of a participatory process will cling tenaciously to this position when they find its effects not to their liking? Some will, and some will not; it is a difficult decision, involving a conflict — and therefore some trade-off — of basic values.

And, finally, what is the alternative? Having reached a tentative conclusion about the benefits and costs of participation *per se*, one must review them in the light of alternative arrangements. Participation may be imperfect, may have its drawbacks, but still be a better policy than doing without it. The problem is not simply who is affected by participation and how, but also who is affected by its absence. The question of alternatives opens up a hornet's nest of new problems, for it raises the basic issue of what participation is for. Different answers give rise to different alternatives. If participation is seen primarily as a means of increasing consumer influence over services, for instance, one alternative is to introduce a greater measure of consumer choice, as suggested by those advocating voucher schemes. If it is seen primarily as a means of reducing arbitrary decisions by service-providers, on the other hand, one alternative is to reduce the amount of bureaucratic discretion, as advocated by those pressing for more welfare rights. If participation is seen, however, as a means of involving people in activity and discussions, then these alternatives have little relevance, and suggestions need to be put forward for engaging people in other ways. Participation in social policy issues is not the only way of achieving any single aim, but other courses of action depend on which aim one has in mind. But these cannot be fully explored here; they deserve books of their own.

In conclusion, it is obvious that there is no single 'correct' view on participation, whoever it is supposed to involve and for whatever purpose. The tides of fashion will ebb and flow, bringing participation now to public attention and removing it now from all consideration, but little consensus will ever be reached about why it is or is not desirable. There will be those who seek to involve others, those who seek to become involved themselves and those who hope never to be asked to participate at all. These are all political stances, stemming from fundamental political attitudes and assumptions — for politics, in the final analysis, is what participation is all about.

Notes

Full details on the works cited below will be found in the appropriate entry in the bibliography.

2 The concept and forms of participation

1 Sidney Verba, Norman H. Nie and Jae-on Kim, *Participation and Political Equality*, p. 46.
2 For a full discussion of these and other issues see Hanna Fenichel Pitkin, *The Concept of Representation*.
3 Edward N. Muller, *Aggressive Political Participation*, 1979.
4 Samuel H. Barnes and Max Kaase, *Political Participation*, 1979.
5 See discussion in Dennis C. Mueller, *Public Choice*, p. 66.
6 See, for instance, the report of the Plowden Committee — Department of Education and Science, *Children and their Primary Schools*, 1967 — and of the Seebohm Committee — Committee on Local Authority and Allied Personal Social Services, *Report*, 1968.
7 Verba *et al.*, *op. cit.*, p. 47.
8 *Ibid.*, p. 47.
9 Sidney Verba, *Small Groups and Political Behaviour*, p. 220; see also p. 224.
10 Carole Pateman, *Participation and Democratic Theory*, p. 68.
11 *Ibid.* pp. 70-1.
12 *Ibid.* p. 70 footnote.
13 Geraint Parry, 'The idea of political participation', in Geraint Parry, ed., *Participation in Politics*, p. 16.
14 *Ibid.* p. 16.
15 P. H. Partridge, 'Some notes on the concept of power', *Political Studies*, p. 116.
16 See, for instance, Robert A. Dahl, *Who Governs?* for one of the principal protagonists of this point of view.
17 Peter Bachrach and Morton S. Baratz, *Power and Poverty*, p. 44.
18 Steven Lukes, *Power: A Radical View*, p. 23.

3 Recent initiatives in participation in social policy

1 National Health Service Reorganisation Act 1973, Part 1, section 9.
2 For a fuller discussion, see Rudolf Klein and Janet Lewis, *The Politics of Consumer Representation: A Study of Community Health Councils*, London, Centre for Studies in Social Policy, 1976.
3 Shirley Williams in House of Commons debates, 1 July 1971, quoted in R. G. S. Brown, *Reorganising the National Health Service*, Oxford, Basil Blackwell, 1979, p. 29.
4 Royal Commission on the National Health Service, *Report*, 1979.
5 Department of Health and Social Security, *Patients First*, London, HMSO, 1979.
6 See the DHSS circular HC(81)15 for a discussion of the position at time of writing.
7 *British Medical Journal*, vol. 282, 2 May 1981, p. 1413.
8 Jo Wood and D. H. H. Metcalfe, 'Professional attitudes to patient participation groups: an exploratory study', *Journal of the Royal College of General Practitioners*, no. 30, September 1980, p. 539.
9 Royal Commission on the National Health Service, *op. cit.*, p. 156.
10 1980 *Housing Act*, Part 1, Ch. II, section 43.
11 See Ann Richardson, 'Decision-making by non-elected members: an analysis of new provisions in the *1972 Local Government Act*', *Journal of Social Policy*, vol. 6, no. 2.
12 See Ann Richardson, 'The Politics of Participation: A Study of Schemes for Tenant Participation in Council Housing Management', unpublished Ph.D dissertation, London School of Economics, University of London, 1977.
13 Department of the Environment, *Housing Policy: A Consultative Document*, London, HMSO, 1977.
14 Department of the Environment, *Getting Tenants Involved*, London, DOE, 1977.
15 Department of the Environment, *Final Report of the Working Party on Housing Cooperatives*, London, HMSO, 1975.
16 Quoted in *The Times*, 14 Jan. 1981.
17 See 1980 *Education Act*, Section 2.
18 Department of Education and Science, *A New Partnership for our Schools* (Taylor Report), London, HSMO, 1977.
19 Department of Education and Science, *Children and their Primary Schools: A Report of the Central Advisory Council for Education (England)*, London, HMSO, 1967, para. 1150.
20 See DES, *A New Partnership*, op. cit., p. 10.
21 See Rick Rogers, *Crowther to Warnock: How Fourteen Reports Tried to Change Children's Lives*, p. 253 (the survey was carried out by the Advisory Centre for Education).
22 George Baron and D. A. Howell, *The Government and Management of Schools*, p. 1.
23 Miriam David, *The State, the Family and Education*, p. 206.

24 See Miriam David, 'Parents and educational politics in 1977', in
    Muriel Brown and Sally Baldwin, eds, *The Yearbook of Social
    Policy in Britain, 1977*.
25 Committee on Local Authority and Allied Personal Social Services
    (Chairman, Lord Seebohm), *Report*, p. 147.
26 See Roger Hadley and Morag McGrath, *Going Local*, 1980.
27 National Consumer Council, *Means Tested Benefits*, p. 63.
28 Department of Health and Social Security, *Social Security Users –
    Local Consultative Groups* (Supplementary Benefits Administra-
    tion Papers no. 8), London, HMSO, 1978.
29 See Michael Goldsmith, *Politics, Planning and the City*, p. 140.
30 *Town and Country Planning Act 1971*, Part 2, sections 8 and 12.
31 Ministry of Housing and Local Government, *People and Planning:
    Report of the Committee on Public Participation in Planning*
    (Chairman, A. M. Skeffington), London, HMSO, 1968.
32 See Roy Darke, 'Public participation and state power: the case of
    South Yorkshire', *Policy and Politics*, vol. 7, no. 4, Oct. 1979.
33 See the discussion of this issue in L. J. Sharpe, 'Instrumental
    participation and urban government', in J. A. G. Griffith, ed.,
    From Policy to Administration, 1976.
34 Department of Trade, *Report of the Committee of Inquiry on
    Industrial Democracy* (Chairman, Lord Bullock), London, HMSO,
    1977.
35 Sam Brier 'Breaking the "them and us" barriers', *Social Work
    Today*, vol. 12, no. 22, 3 February 1981.
36 See National and Local Government Officers Association
    (NALGO), *Industrial Democracy*, Newcastle, NALGO, 1977.
37 For one example of such a manual, see Department of the Environ-
    ment, *Getting Tenants Involved*, London, DOE, 1977.

4 The claims for participation

1 Ronald Dworkin, *Taking Rights Seriously*, p. 83; the order of the
   sentences have been reversed to correspond with the order of the
   argument here.
2 Michael Heseltine, quoted in Robert Cowan, Marc Dorfman and
   Steve Gillan, 'The two faces of public participation', *Town and
   Country Planning*, p. 3.
3 Maria Brenton, 'Worker participation and the social service agency',
   British Journal of Social Work, p. 291.
4 Julia Parker, *Social Policy and Citizenship*, p. 153.
5 P. H. Hirst and R. S. Peters, *The Logic of Education*, London,
   Routledge & Kegan Paul, 1970, p. 118.
6 Carl J. Friedrich, 'Participation without responsibility: co-
   determination in industry and university', in J. Roland Pennock
   and John W. Chapman, eds, *Participation in Politics*, p. 210.
7 Geraint Parry, 'The idea of political participation', in Geraint

Parry, ed., *Participation in Politics*, pp. 18-19. The order of the two sentences is reversed from the original.

8   Peter Marcuse, 'Tenant participation – for what?', working paper 112.20, The Urban Institute, Washington, D.C., 1970, p. 21.

9   Edgar S. Cahn and Jean Camper Cahn, 'Maximum feasible participation: a general overview', in Edgar S. Cahn and Barry A. Passett, eds, *Citizen Participation: Effecting Community Change*, p. 31.

10 Sam Brier, 'Breaking the "them and us" barriers', *Social Work Today*, vol. 12, no. 22, 3 Feb. 1981, p. 14.

11 See, for instance, Brenton, *op. cit.*

12 Carole Pateman, *Participation and Democratic Theory*, pp. 42-3.

13 Peter Bachrach, 'Interest, participation and democratic theory', in J. Roland Pennock and John W. Chapman, eds, *Participation in Politics*, p. 40.

14 *Ibid.*, p. 48.

15 David Braybrooke, 'The meaning of participation and of demands for it: a preliminary survey of the conceptual issues', in J. Roland Pennock and John W. Chapman, eds, *Participation in Politics*, p. 82.

16 Marcuse, *op. cit.*, pp. 21-2.

17 George Kateb, 'Comments on David Braybrooke's "The meaning of participation and of demands for it" ', in J. Roland Pennock and John Chapman, eds, *Participation in Politics*, p. 94, italics in original.

18 E. Gellhorn, quoted in W. P. Collins, 'Public participation in bureaucratic decision-making: a re-appraisal', *Public Administration*, vol. 58, Winter 1980, p. 465.

19 Department of the Environment Circular 52/72, quoted in Noel Boaden, Michael Goldsmith, William Hampton and Peter Stringer, 'Public participation in planning within a representative local democracy', *Policy and Politics*, p. 57.

20 John Stuart Mill, *On Liberty*, pp.164-5.

21 Joan Sallis, *School Managers and Governors: Taylor and After*, p. 28.

22 P. J. Dixon, 'Council houses: theirs or ours?' unpublished paper given to the Annual Conference of the Institute of Housing Managers, October, 1973, p. 4.

23 East London Claimants Union, 'East London Claimants' Union and the concept of self-management', in David Jones and Marjorie Mayo, eds, *Community Work One*, p. 88.

24 John Dearlove, 'The control of change and the regulation of community action', in David Jones and Marjorie Mayo, eds, *Community Work One*, p. 37.

25 Saul Alinsky, quoted in Marcuse, *op. cit.*, p. 36.

26 Ministry of Housing and Local Government, *People and Planning: Report of the Committee on Public Participation in Planning*, p. 4.

27 Department of Education and Science, *A New Partnership for our Schools*, p. 14.

28   P. J. Dixon, *op. cit.*, p. 2.
29   Rudolf Klein and Janet Lewis, *The Politics of Consumer Representation: A Study of Community Health Councils*, p. 153.
30   Council of Europe, *Information and Communication about Municipal Affairs: the Use of Various Means for Informing Citizens to Facilitate their Participation*, p. 26.
31   Andrew Leigh, 'Participation in British Social Services Planning', *Community Development Journal*, p. 157.
32   Klein and Lewis, *op. cit.*, p. 158.
33   Geraint Parry, *op. cit.*, p. 19.
34   Klein and Lewis, *op. cit.*, p. 152.
35   Committee on Local Authority and Allied Personal Social Services, *Report*, p. 151.
36   Consumer Council, *Consumer Consultative Machinery in the Nationalised Industries*, quoted in Committee on Local Authority and Allied Personal Social Services, *ibid.*, p. 151.
37   R. G. S. Brown, *The Management of Welfare*, p. 268.
38   *Ibid.*, p. 262.
39   Friedrich, *op. cit.*, p. 201.
40   J. M. Simmie, *Citizens in Conflict*, p. 137.
41   Brown, *op. cit.*, p. 277.
42   Colin Ward, *Tenants Take Over*, p. 75.
43   Cynthia Cockburn, *The Local State*, p. 97-8, italics in original.
44   Anonymous, quoted in Sherry R. Arnstein, 'Eight rungs on the ladder of citizen participation', in Edgar S. Cahn and Barry A. Passett, eds, *Citizen Participation: Effecting Community Change*, p. 72.
45   Peter Saunders, *Urban Politics*, p. 284.
46   Derek Fox, 'Tenant participation — a new task for housing managers?', *Housing Monthly*, vol. 10, no. 1, July 1974, p. 20.
47   Richard Batley, 'An exploration of non-participation in planning', *Policy and Politics*, p. 95.
48   Robert A. Dahl, *After the Revolution?*, p. 44.
49   See *ibid.*, pp. 46-7.
50   Bachrach, *op. cit.*, p. 52.
51   Braybrooke, *op. cit.*, p. 65.

5 Analysing participation

1   Oran R. Young, *Bargaining: Formal Theories of Negotiation*, p. 5.
2   All quotations are from Benjamin C. Roberts, Hideaki Okamoto and George C. Lodge, *Collective Bargaining and Employee Participation in Western Europe*, p. 5.
3   Brian Barry, *Political Argument*, p. 87.
4   J. R. Lucas, *Democracy and Participation*, p. 23.
5   Allan W. Lerner, *The Politics of Decision-Making*, p. 25.
6   L. J. Sharpe, 'Instrumental participation and urban government',

in J. A. G. Griffith, ed., *From Policy to Administration*, p. 130.

7   Joan Sallis, *School Managers and Governors: Taylor and After*, p. 37.

8   Rudolf Klein and Janet Lewis, *The Politics of Consumer Representation: A Study of Community Health Councils*, p. 132.

9   Peter Bachrach, 'Interest, participation and democratic theory', in J. Roland Pennock and John W. Chapman, eds, *Participation in Politics*, p. 51.

10 Robert A. Dahl, *After the Revolution?*, pp. 74-5.

11 T. C. Schelling, *The Strategy of Conflict*, p. 3 note.

12 *Ibid.*, p. 84.

13 *Ibid.*, p. 5.

14 Amartya K. Sen, *Collective Choice and Social Welfare*, p. 118.

15 P. H. Partridge, 'Some notes on the concept of power', *Political Studies*, p. 121.

16 Jurg Steiner and Robert H. Dorff, 'Decision by interpretation: a new concept for an often overlooked decision mode', *British Journal of Political Science*, p. 3.

17 M. B. E. Smith, 'The value of participation', in J. Roland Pennock and John W. Chapman, eds, *Participation in Politics*, p. 139.

18 Sherry R. Arnstein, 'Eight rungs on the ladder of citizen participation', in Edgar S. Cahn and Barry A. Passett, eds, *Citizen Participation: Effecting Community Change*, p. 70.

19 See, for example, Jan Carter, *Day Services for Adults* and William Pickard, quoted in Colin Ward, *Tenants Take Over*, p. 64.

20 Carole Pateman, *Participation and Democratic Theory*, p. 68.

21 Lester W. Milbrath and M. L. Goel, *Political Participation*, p. 57, italics in original.

22 *Ibid.*, p. 58.

23 Peter Saunders, *Urban Politics*, p. 284.

24 *Ibid.*, p. 288.

6 The genesis of participation

1   Rudolf Klein and Janet Lewis, *The Politics of Consumer Representation: A Study of Community Health Councils*, p. 13.

2   David Donnison, speech to the annual conference of the Child Poverty Action Group 1976, quoted in Department of Health and Social Security, *Social Security Users – Local Consultative Groups*, (Supplementary Benefits Administration Papers No. 8), p. 1.

3   L. J. Sharpe, 'Instrumental participation and urban government', in J. A. G. Griffith, ed., *From Policy to Administration*, p. 122.

4   John Ladd, 'The ethics of participation', in J. Roland Pennock and John W. Chapman, eds, *Participation in Politics*, p. 103.

5   *Ibid.*, p. 103.

6   Anthony Arblaster, 'Participation: context and conflict', in Geraint Parry, ed., *Participation in Politics*, p. 52.

7   *Ibid.*, p. 52.
8   David Braybrooke, 'The meaning of participation and of demands
    for it: a preliminary survey of the conceptual issues', in J. Roland
    Pennock and John W. Chapman, eds, *Participation in Politics*,
    p. 72.
9   George Kateb, 'Comments on David Braybrooke's "The meaning
    of participation and the demands for it" ', in J. Roland Pennock
    and John W. Chapman, eds, *Participation in Politics*, p. 91.
10 Madeline Drake, Brian McLoughlin, Robin Thompson and Jennifer
    Thornley, *Aspects of Structure Planning in Britain*, Centre for
    Environmental Studies Research, Paper 20, Sept. 1975, p. 104.
11 John P. Macey and Charles Vivian Baker, *Housing Management*,
    London, The Estates Gazette Ltd, 1973, p. 1.
12 *Ibid.*, p. 264.
13 Octavia Hill, 'Blank Court' (1871) quoted in M. M. Jeffery and
    Edith Neville, *Housing Property and its Management: Some Papers
    on the Methods of Management Introduced by Miss Octavia Hill
    and Adapted to Modern Conditions*, London, George Allen &
    Unwin, 1921, pp. 33-4.
14 The Society of Women Housing Managers, Inc., *Housing Estate
    Management (Being an account of the development of the work
    initiated by Octavia Hill)*, London; The Society of Women Housing
    Managers, 1946.
15 David Donnison, 'Foreword' in Department of Health and Social
    Security, *Social Security Users – Local Consultative Groups*
    (Supplementary Benefits Administration Paper no. 8), p. 5.
16 Konrad Smigielski, quoted in H. Howard Karslake, *Town and
    Country Planning Act 1968: an Annotated Text*, London, Rating
    and Valuation Association, 1968, pp. 8-9.
17 Rosemary J. Rowles, ed., *Housing Management*, London, Sir Isaac
    Pitman & Sons, 1979, pp. 32-4.
18 *Ibid.*, p. 49.
19 *Ibid.*, p. 121.
20 P. M. M. Pritchard, 'Patient participation in primary health care –
    a discussion paper', *Health Trends*, vol. 2, no. 4, 1979, p. 95,
    italics in original.
21 Derek Fox, 'Tenant participation – a new task for housing manage-
    ment?', *Housing Monthly*, vol. 10, no. 1, July 1974, p. 18.
22 L. J. Sharpe, *op. cit.*, p. 126.
23 Michael Goldsmith, *Politics, Planning and the City*, p. 139.
24 Miriam David, *The State, the Family and Education*, p. 245.

7 Some concluding comments

1   Shirley Williams, *Politics is for People*, p. 207.
2   Francis Cripps, John Griffith, Frances Morrell, Jimmy Reid,
    Peter Townsend and Stuart Weir, *Manifesto: A Radical Strategy*

for Britain's Future, p. 157.

3 Patrick Jenkin, then Secretary of State for the Social Services, speech to the annual conference of the Association of Directors of Social Services, 1980.

4 Some relatively recent contributions, for instance, are: J. Roland Pennock, *Democratic Political Theory*, 1979; Michael Margolis, *Viable Democracy*, 1979; J. R. Lucas, *Democracy and Participation*, 1976; C. B. Macpherson, *The Life and Times of Liberal Democracy*, 1977.

5 Joseph D. Schumpeter, *Capitalism, Socialism and Democracy*, p. 269.

6 Robert A. Dahl, *A Preface to Democratic Theory*, p. 3.

7 Peter Bachrach, 'Interest, participation and democratic theory', in J. Roland Pennock and John W. Chapman, eds, *Participation in Politics*, p. 39.

8 Carole Pateman, *Participation and Democratic Theory*, p. 43.

9 Department of Trade, *Report of the Committee of Inquiry on Industrial Democracy* (Chairman, Lord Bullock), 1977.

10 Paul Blumberg, *Industrial Democracy: The Sociology of Participation*, p. 130.

11 British Institute of Management, 'Why Participation?', London, British Institute of Management, 1979, p. 2.

12 Tom Clarke 'Industrial democracy: the institutionalised suppression of industrial conflict?', in Tom Clarke and Laurie Clements, eds, *Trade Unions under Capitalism*, p. 375.

13 This issue was explored at the end of Chapter 5.

Bibliography

Deciding what to include in the bibliograpy of a work of this scope is not a simple task. I suspect it resembles the job of compiling a good food guide; there are the standard books which must be identified, the author's favourites which are 'worth a detour' and those references of no special merit but which happen to cover otherwise barren territory. I have tried to include a reasonable selection from each of these categories. A few works published too late to be used in this book, but which were noted prior to printing, are also cited.

Because some students may wish to read further on participation only in specific policy areas, a few references on each of the areas covered in the text are listed first separately. These are by no means exhaustive, but will themselves lead to other works. This is followed by a more general bibliography, including some references to participation in other countries. Not all writings cited in the text are listed here, but full references will be found in the notes on individual chapters in such cases.

Specific references

Health

Barnard, Keith and Lee, Kenneth, *Conflicts in the National Health Service*, London, Croom Helm, 1977.
Department of Health and Social Security, *Democracy in the National Health Service*, London, HMSO, 1974.
Department of Health and Social Security, *Selected References on Community Health Councils* (Bibliography Series B144), February 1982.
Farrell, Christine and Adams, Jeff, 'CHCs at Work: 1980', unpublished paper from the Polytechnic of North London, 1981.
Farrell, Christine and Levitt, Ruth, *Consumers, Community Health Councils and the NHS* (Project Paper RC5), London, Kings Fund Centre, 1980.

Hallas, Jack, *CHCs in Action*, London, Nuffield Provincial Hospitals Trust, 1976.

Ham, Chris, 'Community Health Council participation in the NHS planning system', *Social Policy and Administration*, vol. 14, no. 3, Autumn 1980.

Klein, Rudolf and Lewis, Janet, *The Politics of Consumer Representation: A Study of Community Health Councils*, London, Centre for Studies in Social Policy, 1976.

Levitt, Ruth, *The People's Voice in the NHS: Community Health Councils after Five Years*, London, King Edward's Hospital Fund for London, 1980.

Paine, Tim, 'Patient Participation in the United Kingdom: A Survey', mimeographed, 1982.

Phillips, David, 'Community Health Councils', in Kathleen Jones, ed., *The Yearbook of Social Policy in Britain 1974*, London, Routledge & Kegan Paul, 1975.

Pritchard, Peter, 'Patient participation in general practice: the case for it', in John Fry, ed., *Common Dilemmas in Family Medicine*, Lancaster, MTP Press, 1982.

Pritchard, Peter, 'Patient participation in primary health care – a discussion paper', *Health Trends*, vol. 11, no. 4, 1979.

Royal College of General Practitioners, *Patient Participation in General Practice* (Occasional Paper 17), London, RCGPs, 1981.

Royal Commission on the National Health Service, *Report*, London, HMSO, 1979.

Shaw, Ian, 'General practice and the consumer', *Hospital and Health Services Review*, Feb. 1980.

Weller, Douglas, 'Community Health Councils and Planning in the National Health Service', Birmingham, Health Services Management Centre, University of Birmingham, no date.

Welsh Consumer Council, *Patient Participation in General Practice*, Cardiff, Welsh Consumer Council, 1978.

Wood, J. and Metcalfe, D. H. H., 'Professional Attitudes to patient participation groups: an exploratory study', *Journal of the Royal College of General Practitioners*, no. 30, Sept. 1980.

Housing

Andrews, C. Lesley, *Tenants and Town Hall*, London, HMSO, 1979.

Ash, Joan, 'The Housing Act 1980: What to do about the tenant consultation requirements', *Housing Review*, Jan.-Feb. 1981.

Ash, Joan, 'Tenant Participation. Part 2. Requirements of Techniques', *Housing Review*, July-August 1982.

Craddock, Julia, *Tenants Participation in Housing Management: A Study of Four Schemes*, London, Association of London Housing Estates, 1975.

Department of the Environment, *Final Report of the Working Party on*

Housing Cooperatives, London, HMSO, 1975.

Department of the Environment, *Housing Policy: A Consultative Document*, London, HMSO, 1977.

Department of the Environment, 'Tenant Participation in Council Housing Management' (HDD Occasional Paper 2/77), London, DOE, 1977.

Department of the Environment, *Getting Tenants Involved*, London, DOE, 1977.

National Consumer Council, *Soonest Mended: A Review of the Repair, Maintenance and Improvement of Council Housing*, London, National Consumer Council, 1979.

Richardson, Ann, 'The participation of Council tenants in housing management', *Housing Review*, Jan.-Feb., 1973.

Richardson, Ann, 'The progress of participation', *Housing Monthly*, September, 1975.

Ward, Colin, *Tenants Take Over*, London, Architectural Press, 1973.

Education

Bacon, A. W., 'Parent power and professional control — a case study in the engineering of client consent', *Sociological Review*, vol. 24, no. 3 NS, August 1976.

Baron, George and Howell, D. A., *The Government and Management of Schools*, London, Athlone Press, 1974.

Blackstone, Tessa, 'Parental involvement in education', *Educational Policy Bulletin*, vol. 7, no. 1, Spring 1979.

David, Miriam, 'Parents and educational politics in 1977', in Muriel Brown and Sally Baldwin, eds, *The Yearbook of Social Policy in Britain 1977*, London, Routledge & Kegan Paul, 1978.

David, Miriam, *The State, The Family and Education*, London, Routledge & Kegan Paul, 1980.

Department of Education and Science, *Children and their Primary Schools: A Report of the Central Advisory Council for Education (England)*, London, HMSO, 1967.

Department of Education and Science, *A New Partnership for our Schools* (Taylor Report), London, HMSO, 1977.

Fowler, Gerald, Morris, Vera and Ozga, Jennifer, eds, *Decision-Making in British Education*, London, Heinemann, 1973.

Jennings, Robert E., *Education and Politics: Policy-Making in Local Education Authorities*, London, Batsford, 1977.

Locke, Michael, *Power and Politics in the School System*, London, Routledge & Kegan Paul, 1974.

Mann, John, *Education*, London, Pitman, 1979.

Midwinter, Eric, *Education and the Community*, London, George Allen & Unwin, 1975.

Moodie, Graeme, C., and Eustace, Roland, *Power and Authority in British Universities*, London, George Allen & Unwin, 1974.

Rogers, Rick, *Crowther to Warnock: How Fourteen Reports Tried to Change Children's Lives*, London, Heinemann Educational Books, 1980.

Sallis, Joan, *School Managers and Governors: Taylor and After*, London, Ward Lock Educational, 1977.

Social services

Beresford, Peter and Beresford, Suzy, 'Community control of Social Services Departments: discussion document', unpublished paper from Battersea Community Action, London, 1980.

Brenton, Maria, 'Worker participation and the social service agency', *British Journal of Social Work*, vol. 8, no. 3, Autumn 1978.

British Association of Social Workers, *Clients are Fellow Citizens* (Report of the Working Party on Client Participation in Social Work), BASW, May 1980.

Carter, Jan, *Day Services for Adults*, London, George Allen & Unwin, 1981.

Committee on Local Authority and Allied Personal Social Services (Chairman: Lord Seebohm), *Report*, London, HMSO, 1968.

Deakin, Rose and Willmott, Phyllis, *Participation in Local Social Services: an Exploratory Study*, London, Personal Social Services Council, 1979.

Hadley, Roger and McGrath, Morag, *Going Local* (NCVO Occasional Paper 1), London, Bedford Square Press, 1980.

Leigh, Andrew, 'Participation in British social services planning', *Community Development Journal*, vol. 12, no. 3, 1977.

Social security

Department of Health and Social Security, *Social Security Users – Local Consultative Groups* (Supplementary Benefits Administration Papers no. 8), London, HMSO, 1978.

National Consumer Council, *Means Tested Benefits*, London, National Consumer Council, 1976.

Planning

Abiss, John and Lumsdon, Les, *Route Causes: A Guide to Participation in Public Transport Plans*, London, Bedford Square Press, 1979.

Bailey, Joe, *Social Theory for Planning*, London, Routledge & Kegan Paul, 1975.

Batley, Richard, 'An explanation of non-participation in planning', *Policy and Politics*, vol. 1, no. 2, Dec. 1972.

Boaden, Noel, Goldsmith, Michael, Hampton, William and Stringer,

Peter, 'Public participation in planning within a representative local democracy', *Policy and Politics*, vol. 7, no. 1, Jan. 1979.

Boaden, Noel, Goldsmith, Michael, Hampton, William and Stringer, Peter, *Planning and Participation in Practice: A Study of Public Participation in Structure Planning*, Oxford, Pergamon Press (*Progress in Planning*, vol. 1, 13), 1980.

Cowan, Robert, Dorfman, Marc and Gillon, Steve, 'The two faces of public participation', *Town and Country Planning*, vol. 50, no. 1, Jan. 1981.

Darke, Roy, 'Public participation and state power: the case of South Yorkshire', *Policy and Politics*, vol. 7, no. 4, Oct. 1979.

Fagence, Michael, *Citizen Participation in Planning*, Oxford, Pergamon Press, 1977.

Ferris, John, *Participation in Urban Planning: the Barnsbury Case* (Occasional Papers on Social Administration, no. 48), London, 1972.

Garner, J. F., 'Skeffington revisited', *Town Planning Review*, vol. 50, no. 7, Oct. 1979.

Goldsmith, Michael, *Politics, Planning and the City*, London, Hutchinson, 1980.

Levin, Peter, *Government and the Planning Process*, London, Allen & Unwin, 1976.

Ministry of Housing and Local Government, *People and Planning: Report of the Committee on Public Participation in Planning* (A. M. Skeffington, Chairman), London, HMSO, 1969.

Royal Town Planning Institute, *Public Participation: An Issues Report*, London, RTPI, 1980.

Royal Town Planning Institute, *The Public and Planning: Means to Better Participation*, London, RTPI, 1981.

Sewell, W. R. D. and Coppock, J. T., *Public Participation in Planning*, London, Wiley, 1977.

Thornley, Andrew, *Theoretical Perspectives on Planning Participation*, Oxford, Pergamon Press, (*Progress in Planning*, vol. 7, pt 1), 1977.

General references

Abrahamsson, Bengt, *Bureaucracy or Participation*, London, Sage, 1977.

Almond, Gabriel A. and Verba, Sidney, *The Civic Culture*, Boston, Mass., Little, Brown, 1965.

Arnstein, Sherry R., 'Eight rungs on the ladder of citizen participation', in Edgar S. Cahn and Barry A. Passett, eds, *Citizen Participation: Effecting Community Change*, London, Praeger, 1971.

Bachrach, Peter, *The Theory of Democratic Elitism*, Boston, Little, Brown, 1967.

Bachrach, Peter and Baratz, Morton S., *Power and Poverty*, New York, Oxford University Press, 1970.

Barker, Anthony, *Public Participation in Britain: A Classified*

Bibliography, London, Bedford Square Press, 1979.

Barnes, Samuel H. and Kaase, Max, *Political Participation*, London, Sage, 1979.

Barry, Brian, *Political Argument*, London, Routledge & Kegan Paul, 1965.

Barry, Brian, *Sociologists, Economists and Democracy*, London, Collier-Macmillan, 1970.

Batstone, Eric and Davies, P. L., *Industrial Democracy: European Experience*, London, HMSO, 1976.

Benello, C. George and Roussopoulos, eds, *The Case for Participatory Democracy*, London, Grossman, 1977.

Benn, Tony, *Arguments for Socialism*, Harmondsworth, Penguin, 1980.

Birch, A. H., *Representation*, London, Macmillan, 1971.

Blumberg, Paul, *Industrial Democracy: the Sociology of Participation*, London, Constable, 1968.

Boaden, N., Goldsmith, M., Hampton, W. and Stringer, P., *Public Participation in Local Services*, Harlow, Longmans, 1982.

Brannen, Peter, Batstone, Eric, Fatchett, Derek, and White, Philip, *The Worker Directors: A Sociology of Participation*, London, Hutchinson, 1976.

British Institute of Management, *Participation, Democracy and Control: Forms of Employee Involvement*, London, BIM, 1979.

British Institute of Management, *Why Participation?*, London, BIM, 1979.

Brown, R. G. S., *The Administrative Process in Britain*, London, Methuen, 1971.

Brown, R. G. S., *The Management of Welfare*, Glasgow, Fontana, 1975.

Cahn, Edgar S. and Passett, Barry A., *Citizen Participation: Effecting Community Change*, London, Praeger, 1971.

Clarke, R. O., Fatchett, D. J. and Roberts, B. C., *Workers' Participation in Management in Britain*, London, Heinemann, 1972.

Clarke, Tom, 'Industrial democracy: the institutionalized suppression of industrial conflict', in Tom Clarke and Laurie Clements, eds, *Trades Unions under Capitalism*, Glasgow, Fontana, 1977.

Cockburn, Cynthia, *The Local State: Management of Cities and People*, London, Pluto Press, 1977.

Coddington, Alan, *Theories of the Bargaining Process*, London, George Allen & Unwin, 1968.

Collins, W. P., 'Public participation in bureaucratic decision-making: a reappraisal', *Public Administration*, vol. 58, Winter 1980.

Commission of the European Communities, *Worker Participation in the European Community*, Luxembourg, CEC, 1977.

Council of Europe, *Conditions of Local Democracy and Citizen Participation in Europe* (Study Series: Local and Regional Authorities in Europe no. 15), Strasbourg, 1978.

Council of Europe, *Information and Communication about Municipal Affairs: the Use of Various Means for Informing Citizens to Facilitate their Participation* (Study Series: Local and Regional

Authorities in Europe, no. 17), Strasbourg, 1979.

Council of Europe, *Methods of Consulting Citizens on Municipal Affairs* (Study Series: Local and Regional Authorities in Europe, no. 18), Strasbourg, 1979.

Cripps, Francis, Griffith, John, Morrell, Frances, Reid, Jimmy, Townsend, Peter and Weir, Stuart, *Manifesto: a Radical Strategy for Britain's Future*, London, Pan, 1981.

Crouch, Colin, ed., *Participation in Politics*, London, Croom Helm (British Political Sociology Yearbook, vol. 3), 1977.

Currie, Robert, *Industrial Politics*, Oxford, Clarendon Press, 1979.

Dahl, Robert A., *A Preface to Democratic Theory*, Chicago, University of Chicago Press, 1956.

Dahl, Robert A., *Who Governs?*, New Haven, Yale University Press, 1961.

Dahl, Robert A., *After the Revolution?*, New Haven, Yale University Press, 1970.

Dahrendorf, Rolf, *The New Liberty*, London, Routledge & Kegan Paul, 1975.

Daniel, W. W. and McIntosh, Neil, *The Right to Manage?* (PEP Report), London, Macdonald, 1972.

Darke, Roy and Walker, Ray, eds, *Local Government and the Public*, London, Leonard Hill, 1977.

Davies, Jon Gower, *The Evangelist Bureaucrat*, London, Tavistock, 1972.

Dearlove, John, *The Politics of Policy in Local Government*, Cambridge, Cambridge University Press, 1973.

de Crespigny, Anthony and Minoque, Kenneth, *Contemporary Political Philosophers*, London, Methuen, 1976.

Department of Trade, *Report of the Committee of Inquiry on Industrial Democracy*, (Chairman, Lord Bullock), London, HMSO, 1977.

Downs, Anthony, *An Economic Theory of Democracy*, New York, Harper & Row, 1957.

Dworkin, Ronald, *Taking Rights Seriously*, London, Gerald Duckworth, 1977.

Eckstein, Harry, *Pressure Group Politics*, London, George Allen & Unwin, 1960.

Garrett, John, *Managing the Civil Service*, London, Heinemann, 1980.

Gibson, Tony, *People Power*, Harmondsworth, Penguin Books, 1979.

Gilbert, Neil and Specht, Harry, *Dynamics of Community Planning*, Cambridge, Mass., Ballinger, 1977.

Griffith, J. A. G., ed., *From Policy to Administration: Essays in Honour of William A. Robson*, London, George Allen & Unwin, 1976.

Hadley, Roger and Hatch, Stephen, *Social Welfare and the Failure of the State: Centralised Social Services and Participatory Alternatives*, London, George Allen & Unwin, 1981.

Hain, Peter, *Neighbourhood Participation*, London, Temple Smith, 1980.

Hall, P., Lord, H., Parker, R. and Webb, A., *Change, Choice and Conflict in Social Policy*, London, Heinemann, 1975.

Hampton, William, *Democracy and Community: A Study of Politics in Sheffield*, London, Oxford University Press, 1970.

Harris, Ralph and Seldon, Arthur, *Over-ruled on Welfare*, London, Institute of Economic Affairs, 1979.

Hatch, Stephen, ed., *Towards Participation in Local Services*, London, Fabian Society, 1973.

Hill, Dilys, M., *Participating in Local Affairs*, Harmondsworth, Penguin, 1972.

Hill, Dilys, M., *Democratic Theory and Local Government*, London, George Allen & Unwin, 1974.

Hirshman, Albert A., *Exit, Voice and Loyalty*, Cambridge, Mass., Harvard University Press, 1970.

Johnson, Terence J., *Professions and Power*, London, Macmillan, 1972.

Jones, David and Mayo, Marjorie, eds, *Community Work: One*, London, Routledge & Kegan Paul, 1974.

Jones, David and Mayo, Marjorie, eds, *Community Work: Two*, London, Routledge & Kegan Paul, 1975.

Kramer, Ralph, M., *Participation of the Poor*, Englewood Cliffs, Prentice-Hall, 1969.

Krantz, Harry, *The Participatory Bureaucracy*, London, Lexington Books, 1976.

Langdon, Stuart, ed., *Citizen Participation in America*, Lexington, Mass., Lexington Books, 1978.

Lapping, Brian and Radice, Giles, eds, *More Power to the People* (Young Fabian Essays on Democracy in Britain), London, Longmans, Green, 1968.

Lerner, Allan W., *The Politics of Decision-Making*, London, Sage, 1976.

Lindblom, Charles E., *The Intelligence of Democracy*, New York, Free Press, 1965.

Lipsky, Michael, 'Protest as a political resource', *American Political Science Review*, vol. 62, no. 4, Dec. 1968.

Lively, Jack, *Democracy*, Oxford, Basil Blackwell, 1975.

Long, Anthony Roger, *Participation and the Community*, London, Pergamon Press (*Progress in Planning*, vol. 5, pt 2), 1976.

Long, Joyce, *Employee Participation and Local Government*, Lewes, Society of Local Authority Chief Executives, 1976.

Lucas, J. R., *Democracy and Participation*, Harmondsworth, Penguin, 1976.

Lukes, Steven, *Power: A Radical View*, London, Macmillan, 1974.

Macpherson, C. B., *The Life and Times of Liberal Democracy*, London, Oxford University Press, 1977.

Margolis, Michael, *Viable Democracy*, Harmondsworth, Penguin, 1979.

Marris, Peter and Rein, Martin, *Dilemmas of Social Reform*, London, Routledge & Kegan Paul, 1967.

Meyerson, Martin and Barfield, Edward C., *Politics, Planning and the Public Interest*, Chicago, Free Press, 1955.

Milbrath, Lester W. and Goel, M. L., *Political Participation*, Chicago, Rand McNally College (2nd edition), 1977.

Mill, John Stuart, *On Liberty, On Representative Government*, London, Everyman's Library edition, Dent, 1960.

Mueller, Dennis C., *Public Choice*, Cambridge, Cambridge University Press, 1979.

Muller, Edward N., *Aggressive Participation*, Princeton, New Jersey, Princeton University Press, 1979.

National and Local Government Officers Association (NALGO), *Industrial Democracy*, Newcastle, NALGO, 1977.

National Consumer Council, *Consumers and the Nationalised Industries*, London, HMSO, 1976.

Olson, Mancur, Jr., *The Logic of Collective Action*, New York, Schocken Books, 1968.

Organisation for Economic Cooperation and Development, *Workers' Participation*, Paris, OECD, 1976.

Parker, Julia, *Social Policy and Citizenship*, London, Macmillan, 1975.

Parry, Geraint, ed., *Participation in Politics*, Manchester, Manchester University Press, 1972.

Partridge, P. H., 'Some notes on the concept of power', *Political Studies*, vol. 11, no. 2, June 1963.

Pateman, Carole, *Participation and Democratic Theory*, Cambridge, Cambridge University Press, 1970.

Pennock, J. Roland, *Democratic Political Theory*, Princeton, New Jersey, Princeton University Press, 1979.

Pennock, J. Roland and Chapman, John W., eds, *Participation in Politics* (Nomos XVI), New York, Leiber-Atherton, 1975.

Pickvance, C. G., ed., *Urban Sociology*, London, Tavistock, 1976.

Pitkin, Hanna Fenichel, *The Concept of Representation*, Berkeley, University of California Press, 1967.

Robson, William and Crick, Bernard, *The Future of the Social Services*, Harmondsworth, Penguin, 1970.

Rose, Hilary, 'Participation: The icing on the welfare cake?' in Kathleen Jones, ed., *The Yearbook of Social Policy 1975*, London, Routledge & Kegan Paul, 1975.

Rowe, Andrew, *Democracy Renewed*, London, Sheldon Press, 1975.

Rowe, Andrew, 'Participation and the voluntary sector: the independent contribution', *Journal of Social Policy*, vol. 7, no. 1, Jan. 1978.

Saunders, Peter, *Urban Politics*, Harmondsworth, Penguin, 1980.

Schelling, T. C., *The Strategy of Conflict*, New York, Oxford University Press, 1960.

Schumpeter, Joseph A., *Capitalism, Socialism and Democracy*, New York, Harper & Row, 1962.

Sen, Amartya K., *Collective Choice and Social Welfare*, San Francisco, Holden Day, 1970.

Sharpe, L. J., ed., *Decentralist Trends in Western Democracies*, London, Sage, 1979.

Simmie, J. M., *Citizens in Conflict*, London, Hutchinson, 1974.

Smith, Leo and Jones, David eds, *Deprivation, Participation and Community Action*, London, Routledge & Kegan Paul, 1981.

Specht, Harry, 'The grass roots and government in social planning and community organisation', *Administration in Social Work*, vol. 2, no. 3, Fall, 1978.

Thompson, Dennis F., *The Democratic Citizen*, Cambridge, Cambridge University Press, 1970.

Verba, Sidney, *Small Groups and Political Behaviour*, Princeton, New Jersey, Princeton University Press, 1961.

Verba, Sidney, Nie, Norman H., *Participation in America: Political Democracy and Social Equality*, New York, Harper & Row, 1972.

Verba, Sidney, Nie, Norman H. and Kim, Jae-on, *Participation and Political Equality*, Cambridge, Cambridge University Press, 1978.

Williams, Shirley, *Politics is for People*, Harmondsworth, Penguin, 1981.

Young, Ken, ed., *Essays in the Study of Urban Politics*, London, Macmillan Press, 1975.

Young, Oran R., *Bargaining: Formal Theories of Negotiation*, Urbana, University of Illinois Press, 1975.

Index

In the interest of clarity and simplicity, I have been very sparing in my attribution of quotations throughout this text. In order to make amends to authors who may feel unduly slighted, all those quoted are indexed below irrespective of whether their names appear on the page in question.